INVENTING
GEORGE WASHINGTON

INVENTING GEORGE WASHINGTON

*America's Founder,
in Myth and Memory*

EDWARD G. LENGEL

HARPER

An Imprint of HarperCollins*Publishers*
www.harpercollins.com

ISBN 978-0-06-166258-4
Book Club Edition

To W. W. Abbot:
Gentleman, Scholar, Mentor, Friend

CONTENTS

PREFACE

*The most outrageous lies that can be invented will find
believers if a man only tells them with all his might.*
—MARK TWAIN

GEORGE WASHINGTON'S DEATH ON December 14, 1799,
dealt a dreadful blow to public morale, leaving Americans
feeling leaderless, orphaned, and insecure. For three decades,
through war and peace, they had depended on him to see
them through every trial. With his departure at the cusp of a
new century, the nation seemed adrift and helpless in a world
once again at war. They needed to believe that he was and
would continue to be there for them.

The intensity of this desire ensured that Washington
would indeed live on. People wanted to feel his presence, and
so they did. He continued to serve the public on two levels.
In public, Washington's ghost brooded everlastingly on the
national stage, dutifully acting out his eternal role as a symbol,
the Father of Our Country. The private Washington, meanwhile, flitted almost tauntingly at the periphery of the national

vision, always just out of reach even though Americans yearn-
ingly sought him as never before.

Both figures, public and private, were vital to Americans'
perceptions of their nation and of themselves. The public
Washington, memorialized in engravings, marble statues,
and hefty biographical tomes, acted as a bulwark to national
pride. Like the flag, he symbolized the principles that made
the United States both admirable and unique. In this form,
however, he remained stiff, predictable, two-dimensional,
and uninspiring. Ordinary Americans craved a living, breathing Washington, a human being who spoke to them on their
own level but also told them who they were. By nature, he
must be malleable; otherwise, he could not relate equally to
men, women, and children of all time periods and social, economic, and religious backgrounds.

Over time, Washington became a national paradox. The
contrasting and simultaneous urges to deify him as a symbol
and understand him as a man produced tensions that have
played out in every generation since his death. As some exalted him to the firmament, others sought to bring him down
to earth. All laid claim to the "real" Washington, but their
true object in many cases was to cater to the needs and desires of their political, ethnic, or religious communities. In
so doing, they created a series of competing mythologies that
alternatively depicted Washington as old and young, faultless
and fallible, realistic and romantic, pious and skeptical—in
short, every imaginable sort of human being.

It was not enough just to say that Washington was this or
that kind of man; "facts" had to be found to back up the assertion. And facts, like any other commodity, are often ruled by
the law of supply and demand. Nowhere is this more marked

than in the battle over Washington's legacy. From his lifetime up to the present day, cheats and phonies in addition to well-meaning storytellers have capitalized on the American public's insatiable and ever-changing demand for information about his deeds, personality, thoughts, and appearance.

This trend appeared as early as 1775, when Washington took command of the Continental army. At that time few Americans had heard much about him or seen his face, but everyone wanted to know what he looked like. Unscrupulous printers obligingly responded by manufacturing thousands of fake portraits of the American leader supposedly taken "from life," and raked in enormous profits. In the years that followed, and especially after his death, suppliers produced a never-ending stream of stories, artifacts, books, and documents that purported to put the "real" Washington on view, bringing him down to where people could touch and "understand" him. He became something for everyone, a man to inspire, soothe fears, and fit passing hopes and needs.

This faux Washington adopted new habits and donned fresh suits of clothes as he moved through time. Early in the nineteenth century, he conformed to classical standards of balance and restraint, strutting rigidly in an impeccable uniform of shimmering blue, tilting his tricorn hat at the ladies, and consorting solemnly with the august Founders. At mid-century, Washington adapted to the spread of Romantic-era mores by partially unbuttoning his vest, revealing a chest heaving with sexual and religious passions. Instead of doffing his hat in the presence of women, he panted after them with heartfelt intensity, and instead of bearing a nation's cares on the strength of his intellect, he threw himself to his knees and prayed for deliverance. A few decades later, he morphed into a bespectacled collector of trinkets, living a typically cluttered and curiously vagabond late-Victorian existence as he wandered from inn to inn, leaving behind tumbled bedclothes and varied artifacts for future generations to covet.

In the 1920s, Washington adjusted readily to the reigning trends of materialism and skepticism. Renouncing his religious beliefs and pretensions to moral and intellectual greatness, he rolled up his shirtsleeves, plugged a well-chewed cigar into his mouth, donned a green eyeshade, and shuffled stacks of money. He had become a man of business. By the 1930s, however, years of reckless gambling, heavy smoking, and hard drinking had left him as ragged and emaciated as any denizen of a Depression-era flophouse. For the first time, Americans turned away from him. His 200th birthday in 1932 was a gala but passionless affair. People put up his portrait everywhere but shrank from shaking his bony hand. As the years passed he stiffened and slowed, like a run-down mechanical doll, his features growing less animated and freezing finally into a sunken-cheeked scowl.

Americans all but ignored Washington during World War II. Patriotic posters depicted the soldiers of Valley Forge marching side by side with the GIs—but left Washington out of sight. The 1950s idealized the American father but relegated the Father of Our Country to dry passages in school textbooks. Movie screens overflowing with giant grasshoppers and gelatinous blobs spared no room for the victor of Trenton and Yorktown. By the 1960s and 1970s, Washington no longer seemed to serve any purpose except as an image on the dollar bill. A rising, rebellious, young generation that had learned his deeds by rote in grade school drew no lessons from his life as it faced Vietnam and Watergate. He had settled firmly on the nation's shelf, a near-forgotten symbol coated in cobwebs and dust.

I FIRST ENCOUNTERED WASHINGTON at this low point. One of my earliest memories as a schoolboy in the early 1970s is an assignment on Washington that I completed in first grade. My teacher—an old-school type who rapped children on the knuckles for not sitting up straight in their chairs—commanded the class to fill in the blanks on a series of work sheets chronicling the events of Washington's life, and then to combine them into a booklet covered with blue construction paper and a cutout profile of the great man's head. I filled in the answers on the work sheets in accordance with the mantras taught by rote: "George Washington was the Father of Our Country," "George Washington was our first president," and so on. But after I got my assignment back from the teacher, I filled in the blank white profile on the cover with huge, wildly rolling eyes, an unruly shock of black hair, and the inevitable mustache. Somehow I found him more likeable that way.

By the time I entered high school, I had fallen in love with history. Almost any subject appealed. My first research paper chronicled Napoleon's dramatic invasion of Russia in 1812; later, through twelve years of undergraduate and graduate school, I turned to events as diverse as the persecution of "witches" in seventeenth-century Scotland, British perceptions of the Irish during the Great Famine of 1846–52, and common soldiers' experiences of the First World War. I majored in European history but took and enjoyed courses about the history of the ancient world, Asia, the Middle East, and the nineteenth- and twentieth-century United States.

Only one subject remained out of bounds so far as I was concerned: the Founding era of the United States. The briefest glimpse in that direction always revealed to me the same guardian figure—George Washington, scowling in gloomy foreboding—and I invariably turned away.

Self-interest—a principle that Washington understood very well, even if he did not endorse it—nevertheless eventually forced me to come to grips with my old grade-school nemesis. In 1996, well into writing my Ph.D. dissertation at the University of Virginia, I found myself in penury, with a wife about to enter nursing school and two small children. Fellowship money had run out, and teaching prospects were dim. I needed a job. Fortunately, a friend informed me, the Papers of George Washington documentary editing project—of which I had never heard—was looking to hire graduate student assistants to aid in the editing, annotation, and publication of the great man's correspondence. A job was a job, after all, and this one involved history, even if it would force me to spend twenty hours a week in the dubious company of old Gloomy George. I went for an interview, was accepted, and joined the team.

At first the job seemed to confirm my worst fears. Working as an assistant to the editors of the *Revolutionary War Series*, I slogged through piles of letters, memoranda, and reports on every conceivable form of military minutiae—repairing shoes, feeding horses, cutting uniforms, casting cannon, distributing rations, and so on. Washington, far from penning world-shaking declarations or leading phalanxes of cheering Continentals in assaults on enemy entrenchments, seemed to spend most of his time meeting with Congress, consulting with officers, hectoring recalcitrant quartermasters, coordinating wagon trains, and fretting about supplies. There was very little action. Here and there a soldier got drunk and provoked a chuckle, but Washington always seemed above the rough-and-tumble of everyday camp life, maintaining the same aura of cold detachment that made him unapproachable in more modern times.

Spend enough time with any man, however, and you cannot help getting to know him better. That was certainly the case with me and George. At first it was the little things that stood out: the country folk and servant girls who appeared in camp and plied him with gifts of fish, fresh asparagus, and strawberries; the brief note from Martha, written on the day of the Battle of Brandywine, in which she called her husband "my love" and told him about a silver cup that she had just purchased; the rage into which George exploded upon learning that a quartermaster's incompetence had left his soldiers bereft of food, causing the general to pace the floor at headquarters, cursing and muttering; the gentle good humor with which he described the inability of his cook to bake apple pies. For the first time, in my vision at least, the man of marble began to breathe.

Such small discoveries opened the door to the bigger insights that followed. Perusing his correspondence through the bloody battles of the summer and autumn of 1777, I witnessed the foolhardy recklessness with which Washington sometimes threw his troops into battle, almost leading to disaster. In the winter of 1777–78—the famed Valley Forge encampment—I discovered how Washington's tremendous work ethic, meticulous mind, and unshakable sense of dedication saved his army from annihilation, and I noted the tender urgency with which he awaited Martha's arrival at camp and support in his time of trial. Switching to the *Retirement Series*, consisting of correspondence written during the final three years of his life, I watched the Founder grow bitter over political divisions, struggle with the practice of slavery, work his farms, write his will, and come face-to-face with his own mortality. In a process of unfolding, he recovered all three dimensions, becoming not always admirable but fully human. I was hooked.

Upon receiving my doctorate in 1998, I eschewed teaching in favor of staying on at the Washington Papers as an assistant, associate, and then senior editor at the project, spending my days in the company of a man whom I'd never imagined I could understand, much less like. Even as I labored over Washington's correspondence in collaboration with the other project editors, I became aware of a new current in society: Americans had regained their interest in George Washington. Thanks in part to the imaginative and refreshingly unscrupulous work of historian James Thomas Flexner, who had published a multivolume popular biography of Washington in the late 1960s and early 1970s, along with the resurgence of old-school patriotic nationalism after the election of President Ronald Reagan in 1980, the Founder had recovered his relevance. For the first time in many decades, Americans felt a need to know and understand the man who had won their independence.

Unfortunately, much of the enthusiasm was misdirected. Instead of encountering the Founder in his own words through his correspondence, which was now being gathered and published in toto for the first time, Americans seemed satisfied to reach for the old doll that had lain neglected since the 1930s, dust it off, and force it into a new suit of clothes. It was the same story all over again. Old myths last current in the nineteenth century were resurrected and modified to suit modern needs, and new myths emerged: Washington the libertarian, Washington the hophead, Washington the evangelist (or secularist), and Washington, scion of the New Age.

One day, a man wrote the Washington Papers project claiming that he was the Founder's reincarnation, and offered to help the editors make sense of his antecedent's correspondence. Appropriately, he lived in Cincinnati. On another occasion, a well-dressed delegation of Washington enthusiasts appeared at the project and asked to speak to the then editor in chief, Professor Bill Abbot, in his office. Not until he welcomed them in and asked them to sit down did they reveal that they were spiritualists who had established contact with the great man's spirit as it drifted about through the cosmic ether. By then they were seated comfortably, and Professor Abbot had no choice but to let them speak their mind—which took the rest of the afternoon—before they could be persuaded to leave. And in the late 1990s, a reporter from a British tabloid newspaper contacted me to let me know that a portion of Washington's Revolutionary War diaries had been discovered in a Scottish castle. They contained, the reporter claimed, irrefutable information that Washington had received valuable assistance from a race of beings he called the "Greenskins" who lived in a large metallic globe in the woods at Valley Forge—space aliens.

More prosaically, the project was besieged—as it continues to be—with reports of politicians quoting phony dictums from George Washington; family legends; forged documents, which have become increasingly high-tech; and myths and legends of all varieties. They have all the qualities of farce and pathos—sheer comic insanity, and tragically misleading conceptions of the history and nature of Washington and the United States. And they are pervasive. Although many excellent books about the Founder and his era have been published in recent years, there are few—precious few—that do not include, usually inadvertently, some elements of mythology both vintage and modern. Washington apocrypha has become so thoroughly entangled in history and folklore that it is often impossible to identify, let alone disprove.

This book does not aspire to peel away these layers of myth and restore the "authentic" Washington to our view. Instead, it looks at Washington myths, and mythmakers, and traces the means by which they have defined and redefined the Founder from the beginning of the nineteenth century up to the present day. Their stories hold tremendous appeal. Among other adventures, Washington chopped down a cherry tree, wrestled with strongmen, romped with beautiful women, submitted to full-immersion baptism in a half-frozen river, fainted at the feet of a British general, battled Apache Indians, led a charge at the Battle of Gettysburg, chatted amiably with his own astral projection, and consorted with winsome space aliens. In reflecting the needs and desires they were intended to fill, these myths often reveal more about us than they do about Washington. In the twenty-first century, as in the nineteenth, Americans define themselves in direct correlation to their knowledge— accurate or inaccurate—of the Founder.

Inventing
George Washington

CHAPTER I

Washington Lives, Dies, and Is Reborn

IN THE AUTUMN OF 1776, deep in the times that tried men's souls, the American Revolution verged on failure. Stunned by a series of crushing defeats and demoralized by their continuing lack of supplies, the soldiers of the Continental army had come to loathe the war. They no longer believed in themselves, their officers, or their supreme commander, George Washington. They wanted to go home. Their enemy, the British, by contrast, exuded confidence and strength. They had captured New York City and were poised to take Philadelphia. The war, they thought, should end by Christmas.

British general Charles Cornwallis enjoyed the thrill of the chase, especially in pursuit of such a worthy adversary. Washington thought one step ahead of his pursuers, moved unpredictably, and fought savagely at bay. But every day he grew weaker. Moving north from Manhattan and west across

New Jersey, his army shed stragglers as a wounded animal drips blood. Cornwallis closely followed this human spoor, giving the Americans scant opportunity to catch their breath, and awaiting his moment to strike.

Pausing at the Hudson River in mid-November, Washington committed a near-fatal error. He detached 3,000 of his best Continental troops and ordered them to garrison Fort Washington on the river's east bank while he crossed with the remainder of his army into New Jersey. His generals told him the fort was impregnable. They were wrong. On the morning of November 16, thousands of British and German mercenary troops lunged out of the mist and vaulted the flimsy ramparts, forcing the garrison to surrender after only a few hours. The Germans proceeded to beat their prisoners senseless, but Cornwallis had no eye for such cruel entertainment. A scout had brought him an important report. On the opposite riverbank in New Jersey, the Americans still held Fort Lee. During the battle, several figures had been visible milling about the fort's ramparts and peering through their spyglasses. Among them, the scout had identified the unmistakable towering figure of the American commander in chief.

Fox in sight, Cornwallis gave chase. Gathering several battalions of infantry, he herded them into flatboats, paddled across the river to the New Jersey shore, and marched vigorously on Fort Lee. He found it looking like an anthill that somebody had stomped on. Cannon and piles of equipment lay everywhere, scattered amid burning campfires and empty tents. Sick and dying soldiers lay on the grass in rows, surrounded by a tattered, sullen crowd of deserters, camp women, and nondescript civilians.

Once again, Washington had slipped away. Judging from the mess he had left behind, however, he seemed near the end of his tether. As the British sifted through their booty and rounded up prisoners, one of Cornwallis's officers, an American loyalist, pulled aside a mulatto attired in the regalia of an officer's servant. After a few minutes' interrogation the man admitted his identity. He was Billy Lee, Washington's personal manservant. His master, he said, had fled at the first sign of Cornwallis's approach, abandoning his servants and even his personal possessions. These included a small portmanteau, which Lee gladly handed over.

As Lee shuffled off to rejoin the other prisoners, the loyalist opened the portmanteau and peered inside. On top he found stockings, shirts, and undergarments. Gingerly setting these aside, he pulled out a well-thumbed almanac and, more interesting, a bundle of letters. Written from Washington to his wife, stepson, and farm manager, they appeared at first glance to deal with routine farm and family matters. But there was more. With a sneer, the loyalist realized that Washington had little to say in these letters about patriotism, freedom, or military duty. Instead he whined incessantly, splotching the papers with tearstains as he wondered when the war would end and worried about his fate. The American commander in chief bore little in common with Frederick the Great. He was a simpering milksop, and a British sympathizer to boot.

"Tell me," Washington asked his farm manager in one of the letters, "am I, do you think, more subject to fears than other men? For I will not conceal it from you, that, at this moment, I feel myself a very coward." Congress overflowed with blockheads who flubbed everything they put their hands to, even as they issued pointless rules and regulations that prevented Washington from fielding an army equipped to wage war against "our fellow-subjects" in the British Army. Now with the Continental army demoralized and in disarray, Washington lived a charade, hypocritically feeding lies to the American public in support of a war they had already lost. "Thus circumstanced," he groaned, "can you point out a way in which it is possible for me to resign, just now as it were, on the eve of action, without imputation of cowardice?" Alas, he concluded, "there is no such way."

In a letter to Martha, the general expressed his secret longings for peace. "We must, at last, agree, and be friends," he whimpered; "for we cannot live without them, and they will not without us: and a bystander might well be puzzled to find out, why as good terms cannot be given and taken now, as when we shall have well nigh ruined each other by the mutual madness of cutting one another's throats." As for King George III, Washington pined for him like a child for his father. "I love my King; you know I do: a soldier, a good man cannot but love him. How peculiarly hard then is our fortune to be deemed traitors to so good a King! But, I am not without hopes, that even he will yet see cause to do me justice: posterity, I am sure, will."

Bundling the letters together, the loyalist hurried off to present them to Cornwallis. He had made a discovery that might well finish the war. Washington had escaped capture, but he would never be able to salvage his reputation. Once published, the letters would disgrace America's greatest general in the eyes of his people, and ruin the patriot cause.[1]

* * *

IN TRUTH, most of these events never actually happened. Cornwallis captured Forts Washington and Lee but not Billy Lee. The portmanteau didn't exist, and the letters were fakes, no doubt scribbled by some anonymous loyalist in the back room of a tavern. Late in 1776, a London bookseller published them along with the imaginary tale of their discovery in a pamphlet titled *Letters from General Washington to Several of His Friends in the Year 1776*. British reviewers panned the clumsy fraud, but it sold moderately well, and a year later the letters reappeared in newspapers in British-occupied New York City. Washington and his troops were in dire straits at the time, suffering through the terrible winter encampment at Valley Forge and seemingly only a wind's puff away from collapse. The letters caused Washington no additional worries, however, but rather lightened his mood, providing a dose of comic distraction from grim everyday tasks. "What obliging folks there were in the world," he quipped to Martha.[2]

Seventeen years later, the joke turned sour. In the summer of 1795, halfway through Washington's second term as president of the United States, a political crisis erupted over the Jay Treaty with Great Britain. Federalists supported the treaty, which helped to normalize relations with the British, but Republicans violently rejected it, calling it a betrayal of America's revolutionary principles and a slap in the face to France, which was once again at war with Great Britain. Within a few months, the Federalist-Republican rivalry erupted into a crisis that dwarfed anything seen in America since the Boston Tea Party. John Jay, the chief justice of the United States and author of the treaty, was burned in effigy across the country, and Alexander Hamilton—a prominent Federalist—was stoned at a public meeting in New York

City. Mobs burned or trampled British flags in the streets, hack politicians scribbled manifestos, and radicals raved of the guillotine.

Washington tried not to become embroiled in the dispute but failed dismally. Republican newspapers, blaming him for instigating the Jay Treaty, cursed him for "his cold, aloof, arrogant manner; his lack of intelligence and wisdom; and his love of luxury and display." Thomas Paine, who resented Washington's refusal to secure his release from a French prison some years earlier, penned a vicious "open letter" slamming the president's "egotism" and "fraudulent" character and discounting his role in winning the Revolutionary War. The *Aurora*—the most fanatical of all the Republican newspapers—joined in the abuse by denouncing the president's "self-love" and painting him as a softheaded blunderer.[3]

The Republicans did not stop at name-calling. They wanted to humiliate the president and shatter the air of noble authority that had surrounded him since the end of the Revolutionary War. To that end, they reprinted the fake letters from 1776 and cited them as proof that Washington had always been a British sympathizer. What had been a half-forgotten old joke now became a dangerously real slander. Federalists denounced the letters as forgeries, but Republican newspapers stubbornly continued publicizing them. Washington compounded the problem by underestimating it. Taking the high ground, he refused to notice the slander, no doubt hoping that it would fade of its own accord. It didn't. Through the remainder of his term, Republicans touted the letters and triumphantly declared that the president's silence proved them genuine. Washington finally officially repudiated the letters on his last day in office, March 3, 1797, but the damage to his public reputation had already been done. Angry and embittered, Washington would rue to the end of his life the cynicism with which his enemies had employed deceit "to wound my character and deceive the people."[4]

WASHINGTON UNDERSTOOD THE IMPORTANCE of keeping up appearances. The public's gaze followed him everywhere, and at times the sense of constant scrutiny made him wilt. "From the day I enter upon the command of the American armies," he tearfully told Patrick Henry after Congress elected him commander in chief in June 1775, "I date my fall, and the ruin of my reputation."[5] Perhaps at no time in history had so many people expected so much from one man as at this moment. To create an army, defeat a powerful foe, and build a nation—the burden was incredible. All along the way, one misstep might drag him to ruin, shearing him of that quality he prized above all else—his reputation. It should come as no surprise, then, that Washington grew almost fanatically self-conscious, regulating every atom of his dress, speech, and public conduct with nearly ruthless control. In the process, he became two men: a private, carefully hidden Washington, whom no one except Martha ever really met, and a public, meticulously cultivated Washington, on display for popular consumption.

A devotee of classical drama, Washington was no stranger to playacting. He employed it deliberately. In his worldview, Providence—the Great Playwright—assigned each man a role in life that he must play out uncomplainingly to the end. Washington's favorite play, Joseph Addison's *Cato*, depicted a Roman senator's struggles against tyranny, and he consciously emulated the senator's virtuous pursuit of republican ideals. In the spring of 1783, as hostilities with Great Britain ceased and independence seemed secure, Washington anticipated his role in the coming, climactic act of the national drama. "Nothing more remains," he told his troops, "but for the actors of this mighty Scene to preserve a perfect unvarying consistency of character through the very last act; to close the Drama with applause; and to retire from the Military Theatre with the same approbation of Angels and men which have crowned all their former virtuous Actions."[6] He would speak his lines carefully, and according to the script.

On December 17, 1783, Washington rode in public procession to Baltimore. Congress had convened in nearby Annapolis, but he did not presume to call upon them without permission. Instead, he quietly waited six days until the delegates deigned to receive him into their presence. On December 23, he appeared before them, hands trembling and eyes brimming with tears, and read his Farewell Address. "Having now finished the work assigned me," he concluded, "I retire from the great theatre of action; and bidding an Affectionate farewell to this august body under whose orders I have so long acted, I here offer my commission, and take my leave of all the employments of public life." Washington then handed over his commission and sat down. There was no applause. He had conferred no favors; rather, he had given civilian authority its due. Thomas Mifflin read a short note of thanks, the delegates doffed their hats, and Washington stood and left the room.[7]

The sense of relief with which he returned home to Martha on the following day, Christmas Eve, can only be imagined, but he must have enjoyed a deep feeling of satisfaction. He had accomplished everything the nation expected of him, diverting not one iota from the main path. And the final spectacle had been played to perfection. For the American public, however, the climactic scene had not quite lived up to expectations. It lacked dramatic tension and reflected too little glory on Washington and the people. Back in the 1640s, Oliver Cromwell had won the English Civil War and then villainously shut down Parliament and seized power. Europeans routinely tore themselves to pieces competing for thrones. Why had things turned out so differently in the United States? Surely the outcome had not been inevitable. What the American drama needed was a crisis of Mephistophelean temptation illustrating moral choices. The conquest of this temptation would cast into stark relief the goodness and singularity of both Washington and the United States.

The revision began with rumors and anecdotes by poets and storytellers, who fabricated elaborate stories about how Washington had turned down direct and repeated offers from unnamed traitors to become king of the United States. Washington thus no longer stood as the obedient instrument of an inscrutable Providence, but as "a private citizen, who might be king." The idea caught on because it beautifully illustrated the ideals upon which the new nation had just been founded, and set America apart in stark moral terms from its former European overlords. At the same time, this royal fantasy enshrined Washington's own greatness, justifying contemporary verse that labeled him a "rare phænomenon," "Virtue's self," the "Genius of Freedom," and "th' immortal WASHINGTON."[8]

Washington did not bother to correct this popular misconception. If people were going to make up stories about him, they might as well be positive. Similar tales spread after his resignation from the presidency in 1797 and remained current at the end of his life two years later. Benjamin West, an American painter who had worked in London in 1782 on commission for the British royal court, told an acquaintance in 1799 that Britain's King George III had called Washington "the greatest man in the world" for relinquishing power, a remark that caused the queen to burst into tears. Whether West was telling the truth or engaging in a little idle exaggeration is anybody's guess, but the quotation has become generally accepted as genuine.[9]

By the nineteenth century, Americans accepted the man-who-could-be-king story as a matter of course. Generations grew up believing it and passed it on to their children in turn, into the twentieth and twenty-first centuries. In 1992, PBS's *The American Experience* produced a documentary titled *George Washington: The Man Who Wouldn't Be King*. And during the presidential election campaign of 2008, the genealogical research company Ancestry.com launched a search to find out who would be the current king if Washington had accepted a throne. Their efforts uncovered eighty-two-year-old Paul Emery Washington, retired regional manager of a building supply company in San Antonio, Texas. "Had George Washington ascended to the throne," *Newsweek* declared, "Paul Emery Washington (Joe Six-pack, incarnate) could now go by King Paul, the first."[10]

Washington's supposed decision to disdain the crown also emphasized what he had decided to remain: a man of the people. Like Cincinnatus, the Roman consul and dictator with whom he was often compared, Washington renounced power in order to farm his native soil. In so doing, he stepped down from the august heights to which his fame had exalted him, and became a citizen, an everyman whom any American could look squarely in the face. As if to test this principle, hordes of uninvited visitors from all walks of life descended upon Mount Vernon in the wake of Washington's retirements in 1783 and 1797, sharing his dinner table and tromping about his farm. And though Washington was at heart a private man, he never turned a guest away. Even in retirement, he had public duties to fulfill.

WASHINGTON PASSED THE FINAL HOURS of his life on the cold, blustery afternoon of December 14, 1799, in his bed at Mount Vernon. A long ride through snow and sleet two days before had induced a cold, which worsened into a severe throat inflammation. He could barely breathe, and spoke in a painful whisper. Tobias Lear, his secretary and longtime friend, stood at his bedside, overcome with awe and emotion and anticipating the general's every word.

Determined to meet the end with stoicism, Washington shed no tears and did not ask for comfort. His attitude was businesslike. After urging George Rawlins, an overseer, and two doctors to bleed him white—only inducing further weakness—Washington called for Martha and told her where to find his will. Then he turned to Lear. "I find I am going," he whispered, "my breath cannot continue long. I believed from the first attack it would be fatal." What dwelt foremost in his mind? Martha? His grandchildren? His farms? The afterlife? He said nothing of any of these. Instead, he charged Lear to "arrange and record all my late Military letters and papers—arrange my accounts and settle my books, as you know more about them than anyone else, and let Mr. [Albin] Rawlins finish recording my other letters, which he has begun." Five hours later, after thanking his doctors and insisting that his body should not be placed in the vault until three days had passed—a standard precaution against premature burial—he died.[11]

News of Washington's death spread slowly across the country. Word reached New York on December 20, two days after his funeral; Boston on December 26; Charleston, South Carolina, on January 1, 1800; and Frankfort, Kentucky, on January 9. The first newspaper reports were terse—"He was attacked with a violent inflammatory affection of the throat, which, in less than four and twenty hours put a period to his mortal existence," ran a typical account. People sought details from other sources. These included storytellers and rumormongers, who subjected Washington to the proverbial thousand deaths by fire, famine, and sword. Eventually the newspapers printed fuller accounts, but even then popular tales of the last scenes at the great man's deathbed brimmed with imaginary conversations, dramatic gestures, and impassioned imprecations to God and country.[12]

President John Adams carefully orchestrated the official acts of mourning with proclamations and black armbands, and Henry "Light Horse Harry" Lee's funeral oration to Congress—"first in war, first in peace, and first in the hearts of his countrymen"—was a masterly tribute to the man and his accomplishments. The Freemasons of Alexandria, Virginia, conducted Washington's funeral with dignified pomp. Most Americans, however, paid their respects locally, via municipal ceremonies and religious services. Eulogies formed the centerpieces of these events. Most were excruciatingly dull and hours in the reading, but a few treated their subject with energy, if not integrity.

In New England, many clergymen seized upon the occasion to deliver old-fashioned fire-and-brimstone Puritan-
style jeremiads. Washington the noble and pure, taken away
by the will of God—and beware God's judgment on those
left behind! Elsewhere, clergymen dwelt on Washington's
spirituality and his role as God's chosen instrument. In life,
Washington's beliefs had been ambiguous—he avoided referring to Jesus Christ in his letters, attended religious services irregularly, did not kneel during prayer, and often
dodged out of church before communion. But the eulogists
would not admit any doubt. "Let deists, atheists, and infidels
of every description, reflect well on this," thundered the
Reverend Samuel G. Bishop of Pittsfield, New Hampshire:
"the brave, the great, the good Washington, under God
the savior of his country, was not ashamed to acknowledge
and adore a greater Savior, whom they despise and reject."
In their accounts—which contradicted those of clergymen
who had known Washington personally—the Founder
prayed incessantly, went to church regularly, and knew the
Bible by heart. Their lesson: to reject religion was to reject
Washington—and vice versa. "You cannot despise this religion," lectured the Reverend Abiel Abbot of Haverhill,
Massachusetts, "without insulting the ashes of a man, whom
you are forever bound to love and revere."[13]

Eulogists dwelt on Washington's deathbed scene, which
popular rumor had already established in multiple variations.
Some had Washington closing his eyes and mouth with his
own hands just before he expired—an image that, as they
described it, did not seem at all bizarre. Master of all he did
in life, the great man had mastered the grim reaper also,
and chosen the exact moment of his death. Others claimed

that Washington's physical perfection had persisted to the end, without the slightest speck of decay, and that in death he looked very much alive. Thomas Paine, who had called Washington everything but an ax murderer while he lived, now gloried in the flawlessness of his body. Some eulogists even alleged that Washington's corpse would forever remain incorruptible, like that of a Catholic saint.[14]

Clergymen were not the only ones to manipulate or falsify Washington's image in their eulogies. Federalists, led by Alexander Hamilton and John Marshall, claimed Washington as one of their own, dwelling on his agreement with their political principles. They also emphasized Washington's Christianity as a counterpoint to Jefferson's notorious deism. Hamilton went further, orchestrating elaborate military ceremonies that emphasized Washington's role as a soldier, hoping thereby to reinforce popular support for a strong, centralized military establishment. Other organizations, such as the Freemasons and the Society of the Cincinnati, used funeral ceremonies and eulogies to promote their agendas, and an anonymous female orator in New York City made headlines by daring to speak in public on Washington's importance to the nation's women.[15] His symbolic meaning had already taken precedence over his identity as a human being.

THE EULOGISTS WERE ONLY the first of many generations of storytellers. As America expanded and evolved, men and women would retell the story of the Founder's life, endlessly recasting it for new audiences. The process was nothing new. Washington, a keen student of history and politics with extensive firsthand knowledge of human psychology, knew it as one of the risks of celebrity. All the same, the idea that his legacy might become distorted after his death filled him with dread. What would people say about him after he died? Would they pay heed to slander and lies? Or would he become, like Ulysses or King Arthur, a shadowy legend, ludicrously caricaturing the authentic man?

Washington could conceive of only one means of fixing his thumbprint in stone and ensuring some measure of true immortality: a written legacy. His papers, he declared, represented "a species of public property, sacred in my hands," a permanent and supposedly irrefutable record of his thoughts and deeds. Carefully arranging and copying them out in duplicate and sometimes triplicate, Washington jealously restricted even his closest associates from gaining full access to his papers. When his good friend William Gordon sought to inspect his papers near the end of the Revolutionary War, with a view to writing a history of that conflict, Washington refused, citing the need to keep them inviolate until all the official records of the United States had been properly archived and opened to public scrutiny. David Humphreys, who had served as Washington's aide during the war, approached him in 1784 with the idea of writing his biography, but met with only cautious approval. Washington allowed Humphreys to visit Mount Vernon and consult his letters—under close supervision—but meticulously reviewed and edited everything he wrote, correcting and rewriting anything that did not jibe with his memory of the events. Eventually—whether from lack of energy or out of frustration at Washington's constant oversight—Humphreys gave up.[16]

During his lifetime, Washington guarded his papers as if

they represented his very identity. And after he died, Mount Vernon's shelves and desks groaned with paper. There were stacks of bound volumes and well over 100,000 manuscripts, including his diaries, journals, schoolwork, surveying papers, and drafts and copies of almost all of the letters that he had ever written or received. Washington's friends and family initially agreed on the need to preserve this priceless collection, but within a few years of his death they began conniving in its destruction. Martha Washington burned almost all of her correspondence with her husband before her own death in 1802. Widows and widowers commonly destroyed intimate correspondence with their deceased spouses in the eighteenth century, although Martha may also in some sense have sought to reclaim her husband, who had surrendered so much of his life to public service.

Less forgivable was the conduct of Bushrod Washington, George's nephew, who inherited the remainder of his uncle's papers by the terms of his will. Instead of acting as a steward, he cheerfully obliged family, friends, and autograph collectors with clippings from his uncle's letters. An unknown number of entire letters—perhaps hundreds or even thousands—that he gave out as souvenirs were never recovered. Bushrod also surrendered several volumes of George's diaries to friends, who dispersed them all over the world. Many remain lost.

Self-professed scholars eagerly joined in the pillage. In 1803, Chief Justice John Marshall carried sheaves of letters off to Richmond for use in his five-volume *Life of George Washington* (1805–7), returning only a portion. And in 1815–16, William B. Sprague, a tutor at nearby Woodlawn Plantation, took and kept hundreds of letters, leaving hastily written copies behind as placeholders. Neither Marshall nor Sprague, however, could compare in sheer academic villainy to the arch-plunderer Jared Sparks. A professor at Harvard who became president of that institution in 1849, Sparks was a passionate believer in the "great man" theory of history. Washington being the greatest man of all, Sparks determined to compile the first large-scale print edition of his letters. To that end he begged and wheedled Bushrod until he received permission in 1827 to ship a large portion of Washington's letters to his home in Boston. There he attacked the collection with the zeal of a thresher in a wheat field at harvest time—rearranging, scattering, and literally cutting letters to pieces. Arbitrarily deciding which letters deserved preservation and which did not, Sparks gave away hundreds of supposedly insignificant letters to friends, and tore pages from diaries or clipped autographs to satisfy souvenir hunters. Taking Washington's own draft of his First Inaugural Address, a document some sixty pages long, Sparks cut it into small pieces and scattered it like chaff. To this day, only a third of the document has been recovered. Sparks returned what was left of the collection to the Washington family after his twelve-volume edition of *The Writings of George Washington* completed publication in 1837, but he secretly kept many letters for himself. As late as the Civil War, he was handing out Washington letters like so many bonbons.

Another aspect of Sparks's assault on Washington's legacy was his treatment of the letters that he published. "Through haste or inadvertence," Sparks wrote in the introduction to volume two of his edition, Washington "may have fallen into an awkward use of words, faults of grammar, or inaccuracies of style." In such cases, he "felt bound to correct them. It would be an act of unpardonable injustice to any author, after his death, to bring forth compositions, and particularly letters, written with no design to the publication, and commit them to the press without previously subjecting them to a careful revision." What he actually did was to make his own small contribution to the process of Washington's transmogrification from man to two-dimensional symbol. Sparks not only corrected apparent errors of spelling and punctuation and clumsy sentences but also excised or rewrote witty and colorful phrases. Thus "Old Put" became "Israel Putnam," and "but a flea-bite" became "totally inadequate." Anything that conflicted with the image of a heroic man of granite that Sparks was trying to create could not be allowed to stand. These rewritten letters would form the foundation for many Washington biographies over the next hundred years, and they continue to mislead readers today.[17]

After Bushrod's death in 1829, his nephew George Corbin Washington sold the shattered remains of George Washington's precious collection to the U.S. government. Large-scale plundering thereupon stopped, but the damage already done was irreversible. Large portions of the original collection remain lost or subject to the whims of manuscript dealers and collectors. Even today, some dealers chop up original Washington letters and sell the fragments on the Internet. With each plundered, mutilated, or rewritten letter, the real Washington faded from the national memory, leaving behind a featureless outline that others filled in as they pleased.

MOST EARLY NINETEENTH-CENTURY Washington biographers churned out brief penny pamphlets or clumsy, two-dimensional books of the proverbial doorstop variety. These works possessed some merit, if only in the success with which they diverted an entire generation of insomniac Americans from the temptations of laudanum. Otherwise, Washington's early biographers succeeded only in reducing him to a cardboard cutout, immaculately perfect and dry as a tinderbox. The first book to break this trend, *The Life and Memorable Actions of George Washington* by "Parson" Mason Locke Weems, was a tremendous hit. Originally published in 1800 and reprinted in ever more inventive editions over the next twenty-five years, it contained some of the most beloved lies of American history, including the famous cherry tree myth, and spawned scores of imitators. In some respects, Weems was the father of popular history. A superb storyteller, he knew his audience—and gladly collected its money.

Born in 1759 in Maryland to a moderately well-to-do family, Weems spent the Revolutionary War in Great Britain. He studied medicine at first but subsequently took holy orders as an Anglican minister—possibly, it has been suggested, so that he could avoid military service. He returned to Maryland after the war and served as a minister for the next eight years, but found neither the work nor the salary to his liking. In 1794, therefore, he signed on with the Philadelphia publisher Mathew Carey and became an itinerant bookseller.[18]

An instinctive social climber, Weems had connections and knew how to exploit them for personal gain. In 1787 he asked a cousin who happened to be the son of Dr. James Craik, Washington's personal physician and close friend, to secure for him an overnight visit to Mount Vernon—making him one of the hundreds of celebrity-seeking pests who drove George and Martha nearly out of their minds in those years. Weems traded on that brief acquaintance a few years later by securing Washington's patronage for a book of sermons that he was trying to sell, and in 1795 he reinforced his tenuous connection to Mount Vernon by marrying Craik's niece. Weems rarely saw Washington personally, although he claimed to have served as rector at the nonexistent "Mount-Vernon Parish." He understood Washington's iconic power, though, and his work as a bookseller gave him ideas about how to turn the great man's fame into money.[19]

"I've something to whisper in your lug," Weems wrote to Carey shortly after Washington's death. "Washington, you know is gone! Millions are gaping to read something about him. I am very nearly primed and cocked for 'em. 6 months ago I set myself to collect anecdotes of him. My plan! I give his history, sufficiently minute—I accompany him from his start, thro the French & Indian & British or Revolutionary wars, to the Presidents chair, to the throne in the hearts of 5,000,000 of People. I then go on to show that his unparrelled [sic] rise & elevation were due to his Great Virtues." He would present a wholesome, do-good Washington, but "enlivened with *Anecdotes apropos interesting* and *Entertaining*."[20] Carey didn't bite at first, but he would regret it. The public wanted stories, and Weems had the talent to tell them.

The first edition of Weems's *Life and Memorable Actions of George Washington* was an immediate bestseller, and it went through several editions after Carey joined the bandwagon and became Weems's publisher. The ninth edition appeared in 1809, and the twentieth in 1825. Competitors—including Justice John Marshall's five-volume *Life of George Washington*, which John Adams compared to "a Mausoleum, 100 feet square at the base, and 200 feet high"—didn't stand a chance against it.[21] None of them could match Weems's sympathetic style and easy approachability.

Weems wrote with a voice that his readers could understand, as if he were an amiable grandfather with children at his knee. Young people were his primary audience. It was his "first care," he wrote, to present Washington's merits "in all their lustre, before the admiring eyes of our *children*." Weems also—like every one of Washington's biographers since—claimed to offer the inside scoop on his subject. "It is not then in the glare of *public*, but in the shade of *private life*," Weems wrote, "that we are to look for the man."[22] In reality, Weems did not need to succeed in this so much as he needed to appear to succeed. The goal was not to set the historical record straight but to sell books.

The centerpiece of Weems's biography is the relationship between young George Washington and his father, Augustine. Young George, as Weems portrayed him, was no paragon, but much like any other little child. At times he misbehaved. It was his father's commitment to raise his son properly, rather than any innate superiority, that made the adult George great. So close were they, claimed Weems, that George frequently abandoned his friends to spend time with his "more beloved father." Augustine's guidance was firm but never stern—he ruled "by the sceptre of Reason"—and rooted in biblical teaching. On every page, it seems, the two are walking hand in hand, with the father pointing out moral lessons to his son. The best-known is the cherry tree tale, in which young George remembers his father's lesson about truthfulness and admits that he chopped down the tree. But Augustine could be a gentle trickster, too—for example, planting cabbage seeds in a pattern so that they would sprout to spell the name

"George Washington," thus introducing the child to the idea of God's design in Creation.[23]

The almost complete lack of any evidence for the true nature of the relationship between George and Augustine did not deter Weems any more than it did with the book's other fables: George playing war games with his friends; the Indian prophecy that he would never be killed by a bullet; his mother's dream of him extinguishing a house fire with water from a gourd and a wooden shoe; his prayer at Valley Forge, on his knees in the snow (which only appeared in the seventeenth edition of Weems's book); his rejection of the army's attempt to crown him king; his pious references to God while on his deathbed; and all the others. Weems had heard some of the tales in the form of popular oral legends or as hearsay told by Washington's distant acquaintances and relations. Most, however, probably originated in Weems's own imagination and desire to please his audience.

Weems's motives were not entirely mercenary. Money was the main thing, but if he could impart a lesson or two in the process, so much the better. His prime message was religious. Over and again, Weems emphasized Washington's Christian upbringing, frequent prayers, and spiritual dependence on God. He took care not to sound preachy, however, and favored no particular denomination. Instead, he used Washington's piety as a means of appealing to patriotism and public duty. In the Valley Forge tale, for example, a pacifistic Quaker named Isaac Potts happens upon Washington at prayer on his knees amid "a dark natural bower of ancient oaks," and watches as the general rises and returns to headquarters with "a countenance of angel serenity." Amazed, he runs home to his wife and announces his conversion to the cause of warfare. "I always thought the sword and the gospel utterly inconsistent; and that no man could be a soldier and a Christian at the same time," he tells her. "But George Washington has this day convinced me of my mistake."[24]

The Life and Memorable Actions of George Washington was Weems's masterpiece. His later works—including *The Drunkard's Looking Glass* (1812), *God's Revenge Against Dueling* (1820), and *Bad Wife's Looking Glass* (1823)—never matched its success. It would not be much of a stretch to say that in his life of Washington he had written the most influential book about any of the Founding Fathers. More than perhaps any other book ever written about Washington, it appealed to everyday Americans. Henry Cabot Lodge aptly summed up Weems's influence almost a hundred years later:

> The biography did not go, and was not intended to go, into the hands of the polite society of the great eastern towns. It was meant for the farmers, the pioneers, and the backwoodsmen of the country. It went into their homes, and passed with them beyond the Alleghenies and out to the plains and valleys of the great West. The very defects of the book helped it to success among the simple, hard-working, hard-fighting race engaged in the conquest of the American continent. To them its heavy and tawdry style, its staring morals, and its real patriotism all seemed eminently befitting the national hero, and thus Weems created the Washington of the popular fancy. The idea grew up with the country, and became so ingrained in the popular thought that finally everybody was affected by it, and even the most stately and solemn of the Washington biographers ad-

opted the unsupported tales of the itinerant parson and book-peddler.[25]

Millions of American schoolchildren would grow up with the stories that Weems invented. Abraham Lincoln remembered that "away back in my childhood, the earliest days of my being able to read, I got hold of a small book . . . Weems's *Life of Washington*."[26] Like Honest Abe, most children encountered Weems's Washington through penny storybooks, Sunday School Union biographies, or especially the incredibly influential readers that William Holmes McGuffey began producing in the 1830s. In retelling Weems's stories, particularly the cherry tree myth, McGuffey simplified their morals and turned them into generic Sunday school lessons, putting Washington's piety on constant display. McGuffey also transformed the relationship between him and his father from one of mutual trust and love to a much more authoritarian bond.

"High, Pa, an't you my true father?" young George exclaimed during a bantering conversation with Augustine concerning the existence of God, as recounted by Weems. Augustine indulged George's childishly innocent questions with fatherly good humor and instructed him about the Deity's ways with kindly condescension. At the end of their discussion, Weems wrote, "George fell into a profound silence, while his pensive looks showed that his youthful soul was labouring with some idea never felt before. Perhaps it was at that moment, that the good Spirit of God ingrafted on his heart that germ of piety, which filled his after life with so many of the precious fruits of morality." In McGuffey's retelling of the story in his *Eclectic Second Reader*, by contrast, "High, Pa" becomes "Yes, father," and George wisely refrains from such blasphemies as "an't," or the suggestion that Augustine was his "true father." Instead, George quietly submits to his father's arguments for God's existence. In the end, George falls silent, just as he had in Weems; instead of wrestling with a new idea, however, he merely absorbs dictated truth. "A good impression had been made," McGuffey concluded. "He seemed to feel the force of his father's remarks. From this time, it is believed, he never doubted that there is a God, the author and proprietor of all things." Though it was out of tune with Weems's vision of "enlightened parenthood," McGuffey's portrayal would become more familiar to children over the next hundred years as the readers became staples in schools and homes across the country.[27]

By MIDCENTURY, Washington's greatness had become fixed in the public mind. Americans decorated their homes with his image and revered it like a saint's icon. Orators exalted him as a demigod, beyond the reach of ordinary human beings. "Ye ambitious ones of the earth," proclaimed future president John Tyler in 1837, "how vile and contemptible do you appear when compared with *Washington*." Abraham Lincoln spoke that same year of the "last trump" that would "awaken our Washington" and reprove evildoers. Novelists, such as James Fenimore Cooper in *The Spy* (1821), presented an impeccable Washington straight out of classical mythology, an oak of a man radiating stability and calm.[28]

Weems, who died in 1825, had sought to counter this trend toward deification by recapturing Washington for the common man. He spoke not just to scholars but to real, everyday people, men, women, and children, reminding them that a human being—a George Washington they could relate to—breathed within the marble statue. To that degree, he did the nation a service. But Weems was lazy. Disdaining the labor involved in chipping away at the statue, he left discovery to the imagination. Worse, he set a precedent. Over the next several generations, Weems's imitators produced an increasingly outrageous array of myth, legend, and outright fraud in the name of recovering Washington's humanity.

CHAPTER 2

Washington Turns a Profit

J OICE HETH'S BROKEN BODY exhibited all the effects of a life-time in slavery. Shriveled and weak, she probably weighed no more than seventy pounds. Her limbs were paralyzed and her hands and feet were twisted into claws, the overgrown nails cutting into her leathery flesh. Her teeth had gone long ago, along with her sight, and her eyes sat deep within their sockets beneath tufts of bushy gray hair. She looked a thousand years old, but no one knew when she was born or where she came from.

R. W. Lindsay, an itinerant and feckless Kentucky show-man, bought Heth sometime in the mid-1830s. He thought she might make a good showpiece. Her appearance made people stop and stare, and she was bright and lively despite her physical infirmities. She loved to sing, pray, and talk about people she had known in her younger days, when life had still seemed a little bit hopeful. Though she had a hell of a temper—unruly children especially set her off—she must also have possessed a rich sense of humor. Otherwise it's hard to account for her good-natured acceptance of the new show business identity that Lindsay provided her with. She was, he told her, a former African princess who had been shipped to Virginia and sold as a slave to Augustine Washington, the father of George Washington. And she was 161 years old.

P. T. Barnum first met Heth in August 1835. He was twenty-five years old at the time, a dry goods clerk in a store in lower Manhattan, and a restless wanderer. Desperate to avoid a life as a mere wage earner, he had recently accompanied a traveling comedy troupe as the exhibitor of an "educated goat." The gig had hooked him on show business, and he yearned for a chance to hit the big time with an act of his own. Joice Heth seemed to offer that chance. Over the past several months, R. W. Lindsay had dragged her around the East Coast for displays in dingy county halls and public houses. He lacked showmanship skills, however, and had been unable to turn much of a profit. Now he wanted out. Lindsay's partner approached Barnum, told him about the 161-year-old slave in his possession, and asked him if he'd be interested in taking over the management of her act. Barnum hopped on a train to Philadelphia, where Heth was on display, and went to see for himself.

Barnum found Heth lying propped on a lounge in the middle of the hall, hideously emaciated and unable to move, but gabbling happily of her "dear little George" and his childish ways. Lindsay stepped forward and proffered a tattered bill of sale indicating that Augustine Washington had sold her back in 1727 to his sister-in-law and neighbor, Elizabeth

Atwood. The document clearly indicated that Heth had been fifty-four years old at the time of sale. Lindsay claimed to have discovered the document and then tracked her down to an old Kentucky outhouse, purchased her from her ignorant and neglectful owners, and put her on display as a charity. Barnum accepted this crock—no doubt with a knowing smirk—and told Lindsay he was interested. Bargaining down the asking price of $3,000 to $1,000, Barnum purchased the rights to Heth—in effect, taking ownership of her—and immediately laid plans to turn her into the biggest sensation of the century.[1]

Barnum believed in starting at the top. To that end, he invested every penny he owned in this new project and secured an engagement at Niblo's Garden in New York City, an exclusive "pleasure garden" for the upper sets. Instead of crawling out of the gutter, as it were, he would unveil his act in the very heart of urban fashion and respectability. Snatching Heth out of her miserable Philadelphia lodgings, Barnum tossed her onto a train and shipped her off to New York. She arrived at Niblo's bundled up in a sedan chair, hardly able to breathe from exhaustion, and Barnum settled her in a room over a saloon adjoining the resort. He turned next to whipping up publicity. Hiring a sly lawyer, Levi Lyman, as an "advance man," or publicity agent, Barnum sent out word that he had happened upon the next big thing, the act that would leave all the city swooning. Handbills bearing a woodcut portrait of Heth festooned walls and littered the streets. They dubbed her "the Greatest Natural & National Curiosity in the World," a 161-year-old woman who represented the nation's sole living connection to its Founder. She had raised George Washington from infancy, suckling him at her breast, fitting him out in his first clothes, and swatting him on the behind if he misbehaved. As a crowning touch, Barnum invited New York's most prominent newspaper editors to a private showing before opening the exhibition to the public. After a few moments with her they all became "firm believers" and promised to provide all the publicity they could muster. And no wonder; Lyman had greased their palms with generous bribes.[2]

The opening of P. T. Barnum's first major public act created a huge sensation. The crowds were almost uncontrollable. For fourteen hours a day, from 8:00 a.m. to 10:00 p.m., people swarmed into Heth's chamber. Awestruck, they caressed the hands that had held the baby Washington and inspected every visible inch of her body. Some sang and prayed with her, or watched in fascination as she huddled amid overstuffed cushions and "smoked" a pipe that Barnum or one of his flunkies placed carefully between her gums. Most visitors, however, just came to hear her tell stories about young Master George. Barnum rehearsed her well. With a little prompting, Heth would remember all sorts of lively childhood antics and later adventures dodging redcoats. Some of her stories came, with slight modifications, straight out of Parson Weems.

"Joice, do you remember about the peach tree?" asked a visitor.

"Yes, dat I do, very well," she replied.

"Well, tell it."

"Wy, de boys be playing in de garden—de garden be away up by Missy Atwood's—de boys play, and George be dere."

"Well, what did they do?"

"Dey damage de peach tree very much—break de branches."

"Well, what said master to that?"

"Old Massa Washington be very angry—de boys deny dey did 'em—young Massa George stood up like a man—'Fadda, I do 'um,'—old Massa den not whup 'um."

"Why did he not whip him?"

"Wy?—'cause he tell de truth, dear boy—'cause he tell de truth."[3]

Before long the exhausting work of entertaining guests proved too much for Heth, and she showed signs of collapse. In response, Barnum generously cut her duties back from fourteen to eight hours a day, six days a week. Then he hustled her off on a whirlwind tour of New England. Popular interest remained high, but he ran into unexpected resistance in some quarters from abolitionist ministers, who denounced Barnum's exploitation of a poor old slave for profit and forbade their flocks from attending the grotesque spectacle. Grumbling about the "priest-ridden" Yankees, Barnum changed his approach to suit his audience. His show, he said, was being staged not for unwholesome profit but to benefit Joice Heth and all other ex-slaves, and he issued furious denunciations of slavery at every opportunity. The strategy worked. Ministers released their flocks, and the crowds came swarming back. Lyman, meanwhile, wrote and published a pamphlet biography of Heth emphasizing her good times with the Washington family and the kindness and humanity with which they treated their slaves.[4]

In time, inevitably, the act degenerated into a farce. Heth, obviously becoming addled under the constant strain, began calling herself "Lady Washington" and grew angry with anyone who contradicted her. Visitors treated her no longer with awestricken reverence but as a curiosity or object of mockery. Children especially delighted in poking, prodding, and taunting her into outbursts of temper and then laughed uproariously at her surprisingly virile cursing. Observers found the display increasingly disgusting, and many of the same newspapers that had initially touted the show now denounced it. Rumors spread that Barnum had put on a hoax, and soon people were joking that Heth was a resurrected Egyptian mummy or an "india-rubber" puppet. Barnum, typically, just went with the flow. Instead of trying to defend his act he joined in the hilarity, calling her an "automaton" subject to invisible control. He couldn't care less if people laughed at his exhibit, so long as they paid the price of admission.[5]

The end had to come sometime, and for Heth it was mercifully swift. Worn out by months of ceaseless—and of course unremunerated—labor, she died in February 1836. But Barnum was not done with her yet. Ghoulishly, he announced that he would stage a public autopsy, in which one of New York's most prominent physicians, Dr. David Rogers, would determine once and for all whether she really had been 161 years old. Fifteen hundred people paid 50 cents each—adding another $700 to the thousands of dollars that Barnum had already earned—to sit in the City Saloon on Broadway and watch Rogers cut apart the old slave, remove her organs, and crack open her skull to get at her brain. To the crowd's delight, the doctor finished by solemnly declaring that she could not have been more than seventy-five or eighty years old. Barnum expostulated that he had been bamboozled, and the audience filed out happily. Instead of retiring in shame, he gleefully manipulated the negative publicity that followed by anonymously feeding stories to the press that emphasized his brilliant "Yankee ingenuity" by earning a small fortune in the course of putting over a rich practical joke on the American people.[6] In some small way, too, if only for a little while, he had made George Washington come alive.

THE NINETEENTH CENTURY was in some respects an age of pious hypocrisy, of suffocating bodices and table skirts, of parsimony and poor laws. Yet even as men such as Podsnap and Scrooge flourished in England, America became the land of Barnum, snake oil salesmen, traveling freak shows, and—toward the end of the century—vaudeville. Charlatans came up with imaginative profit-making schemes, and duped people by the score. They did not confine their activities to the street. Politics entered a golden age of corruption where everyone, from beat cops to presidents, could be bought and sold. Newspapers specialized in slander. Businessmen and bankers became robber barons, employing fraud and other forms of crime to amass huge empires. Plagiarism and politically motivated deception made inroads into the hallowed halls of academe. All shared a single goal—to earn money, and lots of it.

Americans saw the dollar bill in Washington long before Washington appeared on the dollar bill. The most obvious means of squeezing money from the Founding Father was in the writing and selling of books. A good popular history, as Weems had shown, could earn reams of cash, accuracy be damned. All it took was writing skill and imagination. A ne'er-do-well and habitual liar who happened to be Martha Washington's grandson was among the first to get into the game. Born in 1781, George Washington Parke Custis lost his parents early and grew up at Mount Vernon under the tutelage of George and Martha Washington. He was a chubby child, and his grandparents—who spoiled him terribly—nicknamed him "Washtub," shortened to "Wash" or "Tub." "Your friend Tub [was] a good deal reduced by diarrhea," Washington wrote to his friend William Gordon in 1784, but "he has got perfectly well, & is as fat & saucy as ever."[7] The adverse effects of the spoiling emerged as Tub grew older. He was a lazy, unruly student, and flunked out of Princeton in 1797. "From his infancy," Washington wrote of Tub, "I have discovered an almost unconquerable disposition to indolence in every thing that did not tend to his amusements."[8] George subjected Tub to strict oversight and discipline, but to no avail. After another failed attempt at school, he sent the hapless boy off to join the army.

Military service matured Tub—to some extent—and after his return he married and fathered a daughter, Mary, who would later become Robert E. Lee's wife. But he remained an eccentric. His home in Arlington, Virginia, overflowed with Washington relics, and he daubed huge, inadvertently impressionistic murals of the great man in battle. He also liked to dress, in public and in private, in Washington's old uniform. Every Fourth of July, he would hold public sheep-shearing festivals, entertaining visitors under Washington's original military tent.[9] He also wrote endlessly about his illustrious namesake. In 1828, Custis published *The Indian Prophecy: A National Drama in Two Acts*. Weems had popularized the legend, but it originated with Washington's physician, Dr. James Craik. In 1770, Craik claimed, an Indian chief had approached Washington and told him that he had specifically targeted him with his musket at Braddock's Defeat in 1755 but failed to hit him. A prophecy thus sprang up among the

Indians that Washington was protected by the Great Spirit and would never fall in battle.[10] Weems's version of the story had been short and straightforward, but Tub expanded on it in a romantic tale, recounting the many occasions during the Revolutionary War when the prophecy had supposedly proven correct.

Custis followed this up with short essays and anecdotes about Washington that appeared in serial form over thirty years and were published in 1859, two years after his death, as the *Recollections and Private Memoirs of Washington*. Custis's tales were an odd mixture of truth, exaggerations, and outright lies. Young George Washington sets out to tame the most vicious horse in the parish and prevails in a mighty struggle that ends when the beast's heart explodes. A little later he is peacefully reading a book under a tree when the most powerful wrestler in Virginia saunters up and taunts him into accepting a match. Washington enters the ring, crushes the wrestler in his "lion-like grasp," hurls him to the ground, and sedately returns to his book. On another occasion he demonstrates his strength by throwing a stone across the Rappahannock River (origin of the later legend that he threw a silver dollar across the Potomac). His mother develops a fear of thunderstorms after a lightning bolt zaps a woman sitting next to her at a dinner table, melting the fork and knife in her hands. After the Battle of Monmouth, Washington employs the "Amazonian" Molly Pitcher as a housekeeper and calls her "Captain Molly." Some of Tub's other tales—about Washington's love of dancing, for example—were probably based on personal observation, but they are hard to tell apart from the lies.[11]

For all the outrageousness of Custis's anecdotes, he ironically failed to humanize his subject. His Washington actually became *more* distant from the reader—less human and more godlike. Anyone who beheld the great man, Custis insisted, fell stunned before his powerful visage. Soldiers playing ball at Valley Forge stopped when he came to watch them, because his presence left them awestruck. Stories from other writers quoted in the notes to Custis's book reinforced the effect. Washington had, said one, "that statue-like air which mental greatness alone can bestow." His entrance into any room created a "death-like stillness," and all eyes fixed upon him as if spellbound. His motions were always careful, slow, and dignified. He never shook hands. He seldom smiled or laughed. He was always impeccably dressed, and abstemious at the dinner table. He was, in essence, a large, well-dressed block of stone.[12]

GEORGE LIPPARD, a young minister-turned-lawyer-turned-mystic-turned-salesman from Philadelphia, proved superior to Custis in his powers as a storyteller and moneymaker. Born in 1822, Lippard studied at Wesleyan University as a teenager and considered careers as a Methodist preacher and a lawyer before deciding that they clashed—or so he later claimed—with his moral beliefs. Instead, he became a hack journalist, writing romantic essays and police blotter reports for Philadelphia newspapers such as the *Spirit of the Times* and the *Saturday Evening Post*. Adopting the persona of a frail, highly sensitive poet, Lippard attached himself to other literati, including the up-and-coming Edgar Allan Poe. The two men became friends—it helped that Lippard dragged the besotted Poe out of the gutter from time to time—and the young journalist's star rose accordingly.[13]

Lippard's big break came in 1844 with the publication of his novel *The Quaker City, or, The Monks of Monk Hall,* which appeared as a serial in penny newspapers. Lurid and trashy, it told the story of a secret society operating from a gothic mansion in 1840s Philadelphia, practicing witchcraft, abducting and ravishing young women, torturing people to death, and dropping corpses into a pit through a secret trapdoor. Shockingly, all the members of this society were drawn from the city's elite. Replete with satanic cackles and heaving bosoms, the story immediately became a huge bestseller. Bound as a book, it sold 48,000 copies in 1845 and another 60,000 in expanded form the following year, astonishing figures for the mid-nineteenth century. Lippard, it seemed, had found his literary niche.[14]

Lippard's sudden fame intensified his affectations. Growing his hair long, he masqueraded as a brooding, Byronic figure, stalking about Philadelphia like a nineteenth-century Goth. His subsequent novels, including *Blanche of Brandywine, The Nazarene,* and *Legends of Mexico,* sold well enough to bring his annual earnings up to a very respectable $3,000–4,000. Literary critics savaged Lippard, dubbing him a master of the "raw head and bloody bones school of literature" who oozed "namby-pamby sentimentalities about the beauty of virtue, and heaven and hell." Moral crusaders denounced him as a purveyor of disgusting masses of filth, although his tendency to end sex scenes early made him "an exasperating master of literary *coitus interruptus.*" But buoyed by his continuing popularity and fulsome flattery from Poe, who called him a "genius," Lippard shrugged off all the critics and prepared to take on headier work, beginning with a series of books on the life of George Washington.[15]

Most novelists had so far avoided Washington, finding it difficult to devise interesting characters and situations from a brightly painted but inert block of wood. "Tell me," William Makepeace Thackeray asked as he struggled to come up with a believable Washington in his novel *The Virginians,* "was he a fussy old gentleman in a wig? Did he take snuff and spill it down his shirt front?" Nathaniel Hawthorne wondered despairingly whether anyone had ever seen Washington naked. It was, he decided, "inconceivable. He has no nakedness, but I imagine was born with his clothes on and his hair powdered, and made a stately bow on his first appearance in the world."[16]

For his part, Lippard expressed no fears about pulling the old man's clothes off. He had already disrobed the Philadelphia elite, with telling effect. Even so, his books *Washington and His Generals; or, Legends of the Revolution* (1847) and *Washington and His Men: A New Series of Legends of the Revolution* (1849) divulged no stories of secret orgies at Washington's headquarters, torture chambers beneath the mansion house at Mount Vernon, or George and Martha cackling savagely as they plunged children into rat-infested pits. Instead, Lippard decided to reinvigorate the stuffy Washington legend with robust doses of frenetic action and mystic miracle working, the latter inspired by Lippard's membership in the pseudo-occult fraternity of the Rosicrucians, or Order of the Rosy Cross.

Let us accompany the pen-wielding, raven-locked Lippard into battle. It is October 4, 1777, and the Continentals are attacking the redcoats at the Battle of Germantown. Musket balls splat and bayonets plunge into screaming soldiers, who thrash and roll their eyes as blood flows freely from shattered corpses—everything, in short, perfectly conducted and arrayed to fit the charnel scene. Washington, meanwhile, rides boldly toward the firestorm's center, oblivious to the mayhem surrounding him:

> "Follow me who will!" he cried, and in a moment, his steed of iron grey was careering over the sod, littered with ghastly corpses, while the air overhead was alive with the music of bullets, and earth beneath was flung against the war steed's flanks by the cannon ball. . . . At every step, a dead man with a livid face turned upward; little pools of blood crimsoning the lawn, torn fragments of attire scattered over the sod; on every side hurrying bodies of the foemen, while terrible and unremitting, the fire flashing from the windows of Chew's House, flung a lurid glare over the battle-field.

British soldiers garrison the Chew House, and murderous volleys of musketry spew out of every window. But Washington rides on regardless:

> Washington dashed over the lawn; he approached the house, and every man of his train held his breath. Bullets were whistling over their heads, cannon balls playing round their horses' feet, yet their leader kept on his way of terror. A single glance at the house, with its volleys of flame flashing from every window, and he turned to the north to regain the American lines, but the fog and smoke gathered round him, and he found his horse entangled amid the enclosures of the cattle-pen to the north of the mansion.

Things have become just a little too hot, even for the fearless leader:

> "Leap your horses—" cried Washington to the brave men
> around him—"Leap your horses and save yourselves!"
> And in a moment, amid the mist and gloom his officers
> leaped the northern enclosure of the cattle-pen, and rode
> forward to the American line, scarcely able to discover
> their path in the dense gloom that gathered around them.
> They reached the American lines, and to their horror,
> discovered that Washington was not among their band.
> He had not leaped the fence of the cattle-pen; with the
> feeling of a true warrior, he was afraid of injuring his gal-
> lant steed, by this leap in the dark. . . . He rose proudly in
> the stirrups, he placed his hand gently on the neck of his
> steed, he glanced proudly around him, and then the noble
> horse sprang forward with a sudden leap, and the mist
> rising for a moment disclosed the form of Washington, to
> the vision of the opposing armies.[17]

And so on. Lippard's Washington is brave, muscular, and
always getting into trouble. At times, it seems, he has nothing better to do than ride frantically around the battlefield,
bellowing random orders and exposing himself to enemy
fire. But he is not the only hero of Lippard's imagination. At
every break in the action, some impassioned, gray-bearded old
preacher emerges from clouds of powder smoke, delivers an
oration on the noble dead and the glories of Washington, and
disappears as the gunfire resumes. This wild-eyed octogenar-
ian, who never gives his name, serves a high spiritual purpose.
As revealed by Lippard in *Paul Ardenheim, the Monk of Wissa-*

hikon (1848), the old gentleman has consecrated Washington to the service of the United States. Now, like it or not, he must follow the great man everywhere, bursting in at random moments to attest to his wondrous deeds. In quieter times, no doubt, he lurks seething in the hall outside George and Martha's bedchamber.

It all begins in the first hours of the year 1774, at a half-ruined monastery along the banks of the Wissahickon Creek near Philadelphia. A family, consisting of an elderly pietist preacher and two teenage children, lives in the monastery, feasting on wild edibles and pondering mystical truths. Before dawn, George Washington stumbles by the monastery to ask for directions. He is clad in black velvet, ruffles, and diamond-buckled shoes, and he is muscular and broad-shouldered, with his head thrown back and his eyes gleaming with the "fire of chivalry"—a man in a thousand. On seeing him, the old man and his progeny collapse to the floor, sweating rivers and trembling in awe. Then, unprompted, the preacher leaps up with a shriek of exaltation and drags Washington to the altar. "Thou art called to a great work," he cries. "Kneel before the altar and receive thy mission!" Washington, unruffled, falls obediently to his knees and swears to fight for his country, and act at all times as the instrument of God. The preacher then consecrates Washington as the nation's deliverer and traces a cross of oil on his forehead while his daughter places a "crown of fadeless laurel" on his head and her brother buckles a sword to his side.[18]

This episode inspired even the most cynical of souls. Eighteen-year-old Samuel Clemens, on a visit to Philadelphia in 1853, wrote that Lippard's story had rendered the Wissahickon "sacred in my eyes," and vowed to visit it as soon as possible.[19] Extracted from his book and reprinted as an anonymous folktale—Lippard frequently fell victim to plagiarists—the story became a staple of Rosicrucians, Freemasons, and many others. Nor was its appeal limited to the nineteenth century. Fringe groups still publish the consecration story in pamphlets and on websites, advertising it as one of many episodes in the nation's mystical heritage that those shifty academics don't want you to know about. "It's easy to view [stories such as Washington's consecration] as legend and fiction," opines William C. House, editor of the website reversespins.com. But "they may be true."[20]

Lippard's other tales of the Founder included "The Temptation of Washington," a recycled version of "The Man Who Could Be King." In 1778, British general Sir William Howe has disguised himself as a civilian in hopes of penetrating the American lines and learning his enemy's secrets. Sloshing about through the slush and mud near Valley Forge, Howe happens upon the American commander in chief— "Washington, the living, throbbing, flesh and blood, Washington!" Washington is praying manfully on a moss-covered rock, gasping for breath as he contemplates the miseries of his troops. Howe listens quietly for a time and then steps forward, dramatically throwing his civilian cloak aside to reveal his scarlet uniform. Washington rises as if he had expected something like this to happen, and chats nonchalantly with his rival. After some gentle repartee, Howe makes a suitably satanic offer: Washington shall be a duke and "viceroy of America" if he switches sides. Washington, stomping his foot, furiously rejects Howe, and then the two characters fade away as Lippard fantasizes about what life would have been like if

Washington had accepted the royal title, or if he had been captured and executed.

Lippard had much more to offer, including a little girl who sacrifices her life to save Washington from a murderous attack by her Tory father, and a time-traveling Washington who tours factories and puzzles over modern improvements. Lippard did not expect everyone to take him literally. He sold his tales as "legends" and made no pretense of scholarship. Inevitably, however, they took their place in popular folklore. A story that Lippard presented in *Washington and His Generals*, telling of an "unknown patriot" who convinced Congress to sign the Declaration of Independence by groaning from the back corner of a balcony, "Sign! If the next moment the gibbet's rope is around your neck," was cited by Ronald Reagan in a speech at Eureka College on June 7, 1957, and has been repeated by many others. Another Lippard tale, of the Liberty Bell ringing to proclaim the signing of the Declaration of Independence on July 4, 1776 (although signing did not actually begin until August 2), became a classroom staple in the nineteenth century, and is still widely believed.[21]

LIPPARD'S SUCCESS PROVED that Weems was no fluke. If you told good stories about Washington, people would eat them up. By the mid- to late-nineteenth century, Washington writing became a free-for-all business, just as wild and zany as any other capitalist venture in that laissez-faire society. It was only natural, in such circumstances, for one of the most gifted writers in America to get in on the act. Washington Irving, the creator of Rip Van Winkle and Ichabod Crane, had never attempted nonfiction before the publication of his *Life of George Washington* in five volumes in 1855–59. His strong imagination and stirring prose would more than make up for any deficiencies in his research.

Unlike Weems and Lippard, Irving had already established his reputation. That made him careful. True, he fabricated speeches, conversations, and thoughts that he had no way of knowing about, but that was generally accepted practice. On the whole, Irving worked with verifiable primary source material and offered considered opinions instead of indulging in wild fantasies. There were a few exceptions—such as his account of Washington's presidential inauguration, which, as we shall see in a later chapter, was based on dubious childhood memories—but for the most part Irving avoided the temptation to test the full extent of his creative powers.

Irving's reticence may have kept him from wallowing in the gutter of sensationalism with Lippard and his peers, but it militated against his success with the general reading public. His anecdotes were interesting but generally pedestrian, and although he did a moderately good job of humanizing Washington, he did not bring him close enough to the earth for everyone to see. For educated middle-class readers and advanced students, Irving's biography became standard. Yet for most Americans, gathered with elders and children at the fireside for a winter evening's tale, Weems and Lippard remained more appealing. Showmanship earned the real money, not the appearance of respectability.

CHARLATANS LACKING THE TALENT or patience to write books found more direct ways of making money out of the grand old man. While forging Treasury notes could be tricky, manufacturing historical documents required very little skill. It all boiled down to supply and demand. In the early 1800s, autograph hounds had little trouble securing Washington signatures and manuscripts. The Founder had written or signed tens of thousands of documents in his lifetime, from letters to discharge certificates, and they were floating all over the country. When all else failed, a letter to Jared Sparks or others like him could easily secure a souvenir. By the mid-nineteenth century, however, supply began to dry up even as the market for historical documents rose. Washington letters cost money—sometimes as much as $100—and manuscript dealers and auction houses did steady business. It did not take a brilliant mind to connect the growing value of Washington letters with America's always inexhaustible supply of suckers and to visualize piles of dollar bills.

Robert Spring hardly radiated brilliance, but to this day his name strikes terror into the hearts of autograph collectors. Born in England in 1813, he moved to Philadelphia as a young man and opened a bookshop. For a time his business remained on the up-and-up, although not very profitable. Booksellers are keen observers of human psychology, however—it goes with the trade—and Spring's sense of intuition was more powerful than most. Deception, he discovered, required no particular expertise. In most cases, the customer was all too eager to lead himself astray. Let him believe what he wanted to believe—that he had purchased a priceless item at a bargain price—and he would cheerfully pay you for the pleasure of self-deceit. The dealer needed only to play along. Spring's talents, moreover, were perfectly tailored to the task of separating fools from their money. Quick and inventive, ideas came to him easily. He also spoke with a charming English accent—which customers automatically associated with refinement and integrity—and although he was utterly unscrupulous, his likeable manners made him an amiable sort of villain.

Sometime in the 1850s, Spring turned the back room of his Philadelphia bookstore into a forger's workshop. His equipment was modest—a goose quill pen, some coffee grounds, a few old books, and ink that he specially mixed to give it the appearance of age. Cutting the blank flyleaf from an eighteenth-century book, he would stain it with the coffee grounds, pen a short message from some famous personage, let it dry, and then sell it as genuine. It did not take long for him to discover that his clients particularly desired letters from Washington. Fortunately, the great man's handwriting was distinctive but relatively simple to forge. Purchasing a few authentic letters, Spring studied them for hours to get a sense of Washington's orthography. He then either traced the letter or used it as a guide to compose a new one, usually a dinner invitation or routine request for information or supplies. His forgeries were far from perfect—Spring never quite mastered the easy flow of Washington's handwriting—but they did the trick. Collectors were undiscriminating, and the forgeries sold briskly.

An unusually astute collector detected Spring's activities in 1858 and reported him to the authorities. Spring was duly arrested, but he skipped bail and fled to Canada, where he reopened his business on an even larger scale. Posing as a widow selling off her husband's collection of historic letters, he sold hundreds of forgeries in Canada and across the border. He returned to America sometime in the 1860s, settling this time in Baltimore, and devised new and even more imaginative methods of duping collectors. One was by writing letters to wealthy owners of fine private libraries, enclosing forged Washington letters with a note requesting the recipient to remit $10 or $15 to an anonymous man in distress at one of several post office boxes around the city—an early example of mail fraud. This turned a tidy profit. Spring next exploited the popularity of Confederate general Stonewall Jackson in England by posing as his impoverished daughter and selling his "papers"—including letters allegedly from Washington, Franklin, Jefferson, Jackson, and even Abraham Lincoln—to collectors across the Atlantic.

Spring's crime spree ended in 1869. Arrested for forgery in Philadelphia, to which he had returned after his Baltimore sojourn, he freely confessed his guilt and spent a number of years in prison before dying, impoverished, in a city charity ward in 1876. How many forgeries he had produced by that time is unknown—certainly hundreds, and possibly thousands. They continue to deceive collectors and even libraries to this day. Although the more reputable auction houses generally weed them out—anyone familiar with Washington's handwriting can usually detect Spring's work at a glance—they continue to appear on online venues, sometimes selling for thousands of dollars. Others have been passed down from generation to generation and are now cherished family heirlooms. Not long ago, a large university library acquired a multipage "Washington" letter as a donation from a well-meaning alumnus. Excited, the librarians placed the letter on public display as a major addition to their collections. Thousands of visitors filed through the exhibit, gawking in admiration. Several months later, somebody finally decided to compare it with genuine George Washington manuscripts, and identified it as a Spring forgery. Scholars cried scandal, but nobody could deny that the letter had, at least, made a lot of people happy. Through the twentieth century, criminals such as Joseph Casey, Charles "the Baron" Weisberg, and Henry Gretzenberger—alias Woodhouse, or Enrico Casalengo, a European immigrant, murderer, and prolific forger—earned thousands of dollars by hoodwinking manuscript collectors with Washington forgeries.[22]

BY 1850, LITERARY PROSPECTORS had found in George Washington their own version of the California gold rush. Weems, Lippard, and their imitators staked their claims in the field of popular biography, while Spring and his ilk wrote and sold fraudulent documents. Professional orators stumped the country to speak on the glories of Washington, and advertisers increasingly used his image to sell everything from apples to kidney oil and chewing tobacco. They succeeded because they supplied a demand. Nineteenth-century Americans idolized Washington, not least because he stood in such stark contrast to the political corruption of the day. But they still didn't feel that they knew him very well. This continuing and even intensifying yearning to touch the great man's cloak fed the clamor for popular biographies, historical souvenirs, portraits and engravings, and all sorts of knickknacks. Washington kitsch had its genesis in the nineteenth century.

Though exploitative and misleading, the Washington profiteers caused no terrible harm at first. Even Robert Spring made a lot of people happy. In the later 1800s, however, a series of writers took George Lippard's sensationalism one step deeper into the gutter by peeking into Washington's boudoir. Their early efforts did not extend beyond the merely titillating, but by the end of the century Washington was well on the way to transforming from an upstanding family man into a syphilitic rake. Worse, deliberate attempts to distort Washington's image for political and religious purposes—and ultimately for profit—became increasingly common in the latter part of the nineteenth century. These deceptions eventually culminated in some of the most egregious and influential Washington hoaxes, many of which remain in the minds and on the lips of schoolchildren, senators, and presidents today.

CHAPTER 3

Washington's Loves

CONTINENTAL ARMY HEADQUARTERS WAS not an entirely masculine preserve. Ladies, many of them both beautiful and flirtatious, could be seen lingering there even in times of crisis. There was Martha, of course, who spent much of the war with her husband, but younger women were also often in his company. Washington's army coterie included many dashing young men with young wives and girlfriends, whose sisters, cousins, friends, and acquaintances eagerly exploited their connections to secure invitations to military dinners and balls. The general's aides, especially Alexander Hamilton, roved the countryside at every change of headquarters and bedazzled damsels by the score. "Here are some charming girls," Washington's secretary James McHenry wrote in his diary after headquarters shifted to a new town in New Jersey in the summer of 1778; "but one of the drums of the guard [is] more a favorite than Hamilton."[1]

Army balls were lively affairs, with lots of good wine, food, music, dancing—and knots of intrigue and passion. At one such affair in the winter of 1779–80 at Morristown, New Jersey, Washington himself became the center of controversy. All the ladies, it seems, wanted to dance with him, and their competition for his hand quickly degenerated from friendly to fierce. Nathanael Greene's twenty-four-year-old wife, Catherine, or "Caty," a gorgeous belle and notorious flirt, grew particularly disgusted with Deborah Olney, another attractive lady who had married one of Washington's quartermasters. Caty, whose husband did not dance because of a gimpy leg, had grown accustomed to keeping Washington for herself—during a recent party she had danced with him for three hours straight without once sitting down—and did not appreciate this young upstart butting in.[2]

The rivalry seethed all evening and reached a crisis after the dancing had finished, when the men and women settled, according to tradition, into adjoining rooms. Deborah's husband, George—a lively young buck, now addled with wine—staggered into the ladies' room, where he was captured and held prisoner. The men thereupon sent an envoy demanding his release, but the ladies refused to comply, prompting Washington to lead a raiding party to take him by force. A tussle ensued, wherein Deborah boldly engaged the commander in chief in furious hand-to-hand combat. In a moment she was in his arms—and he refused to let go! Struggling dramatically, she screamed, for all the assembly to hear, that if he did not release her she would tear out his eyes and the hair from his head. "Though he was a General," she concluded in a huff as Washington abashedly stepped back, "he was but a Man." Defeated and properly ashamed, the men withdrew, leaving George Olney in a blissful state of indefinite female incarceration. Caty Greene, however, was determined that the affair should not end there.

Washington slept off his wine and quickly forgot the flirtatious horseplay of the previous night. He had more important things to worry about, such as the nine-foot snowdrifts that had placed his army in deep freeze during the coldest winter in recorded history. Out of his ken, however, in the complex channels of feminine society, the rumors were beginning to fly. Deborah Olney, Caty Greene whispered to her friends, had conducted herself at the party like a slatternly tart, attaching herself to Washington all evening and then crying out to him at its end in terms of basest disrespect. Gossips quickly picked up the story and spread it through fashionable circles all up and down the East Coast. By early 1781 it had reached as far as Boston, where Mrs. Olney overheard some women chattering about it during a party. Aghast, she whipped off an angry letter to Mrs. Greene, accusing her of spreading malicious lies. "I am not ambitious of nor do I wish the acquaintance of any Person, however high their rank and station in Life may be," she finished haughtily, "who, by *painful* experience, I have found can in one moment; with a seeming pleasure, smile in my face, and the next sacrifice my character."

Caty had no intention of backing down. The scandal, she insisted, was notorious; everyone there had seen and heard what happened, and no one—aside from one of Washington's aides, who could be excused for trying to cover up for his chief—had thought Deborah in jest. General Greene, she reminded her rival, had taken Deborah aside after the party to chide her for her behavior, and there were besides "a number of other circumstances I could relate that perhaps would help your memory." Caty could secure written testimony from any of several witnesses—and she would, with pleasure, repeat her account of what had happened right to Deborah's face. "I think persons who are too proud to hear of their foibles," Caty wrote, "ought to be too proud to make them so public."

Washington, hearing of the fracas from George Olney, who appealed directly to him for aid in saving his wife's reputation, sensibly refused to get directly involved. Instead he asked his aide to pass on word that he had regarded the whole thing as a joke. For him, it undoubtedly was, but the passions he provoked, however unwittingly, in the female of the species were far from mundane.[3]

WASHINGTON DELIGHTED THROUGHOUT his life in the company of attractive women. Handsome, athletic, well dressed, and a magnificent dancer, he possessed an easy confidence and charm that endeared him to more than a few young ladies. Romantic liaisons were inevitable. In 1749, seventeen-year-old George found it difficult to keep his cool at the opulent Fairfax estate in Belvoir, Virginia, because of the proximity of so many gorgeous belles. "I might . . . pass my time very pleasantly," he wrote to his cousin Robin Washington, "was my heart disengaged." Sixteen-year-old Mary Cary Fairfax, "a very agreeable Young Lady," charmed George so thoroughly that he found it difficult to remain long in her company without rekindling his passion for a "Low Land Beauty" with whom he had recently dallied. In mock despair, he wondered whether he would have to retire altogether from the company of young women in order to subdue the "troublesome Passion" that he struggled constantly to contain. At around the same time, he filled a notebook with some remarkably wretched romantic verse, such as "Oh Ye Gods why should my Poor Resistless Heart / Stand to oppose thy might and Power / At Last surrender to cupids feather'd Dart / and now lays Bleeding every Hour."[4]

George's heart eventually healed from the wounds administered by the now anonymous lowland beauty, but his passion for women did not fade. In 1752, age twenty, he fell for sixteen-year-old Betsy Fauntleroy, but she pitilessly rejected him with a "cruel sentence" that left him doleful for weeks. Upon reviving, he resumed his romps, the details of which have been lost to history. In 1754, however, a friend hinted in a letter that he expected Washington to be enjoying sexual delights unknown even to the "Ciprian Dame"—Aphrodite, or in eighteenth-century lingo a prostitute—whom he equated intriguingly with a woman named Nell.[5] And the temptations only grew. By the end of the following year, Washington had achieved enough fame from his exploits in the French and Indian War to have become something of a celebrity, the benefits to which soon became obvious. On July 26, 1755, as George returned from the frontier to Virginia, three beautiful young dames from Belvoir—Sally Fairfax, Ann Spearing, and Elizabeth Dent—wrote to him demanding that he visit them immediately. Otherwise, they swore, they would walk all the way to Mount Vernon and impose the consequences of his neglect.[6] What young man worth his salt could resist this kind of attention?

The romantic adventures continued. In February 1756, seeking royal commissions for himself and the officers of his Virginia Regiment, Washington rode northeast to Annapolis, Philadelphia, New York, and Boston accompanied by aides and servants done up in elaborate livery decorated with the family coat of arms. Along the way, he tarried at the home of Beverly Robinson and his wife, Susannah, in New York, spending about two and a half weeks there in total. The Robinsons were friends, but Washington's motives in crashing at their place for so long had little to do with their charm as hosts. Instead, Washington had become interested in Susannah's sister, twenty-six-year-old Mary Philipse. Tall and buxom, with clear, confident eyes and charming dimples, she was considered one of the most attractive women of her social set in New York. Even more appealing, she owned 51,000 acres of exceptionally valuable land. Unfortunately, from George's perspective, she also demonstrated an inclination "to dominate and to shape others to her will," and however the conclusion of their romance—if such it was—came about, the results in hindsight could not have been altogether unwelcome. Two years later she married Lieutenant Colonel Roger Morris, and when the Revolutionary War erupted they declared themselves Tories and fled the United States for Canada.[7]

Washington's final and most notorious love affair before he married Martha involved Sally Cary Fairfax, the "Belle of Belvoir." Born in 1730 to one of the most powerful families in Virginia, Sally Cary was married off at age eighteen to

George William Fairfax, scion of *the* most powerful family in Virginia. It was an arranged marriage and apparently love-less—they had no children—but husband and wife masquer-aded cheerfully, performing their assigned roles in society with wit and aplomb. No one was more adept at the social niceties than Sally, who employed her beauty and intelligence to great effect as she navigated the complicated world of the colonial aristocracy. George Washington, visiting the Fairfax estate at Belvoir as a teen, was only one of many young men who cast themselves at her feet, but she found him more charming than all the rest, and before long they became friends. Washington visited Belvoir at every possible opportunity and learned from Sally many of the social skills that would serve him so well when he entered politics later on. Sally may have viewed the awkward young man as a project, and she undoubtedly en-joyed watching her lessons in deportment and grace take hold.

In time, the relationship between George Washington and Sally Fairfax transcended the bounds of mere friendship, but just how close they became is impossible to say. Sally spent a good deal of time with George at Mount Vernon after he returned from battle in 1755, and with her husband absent in Great Britain at the time there was plenty of opportunity for the two to engage in an affair. George most likely fell in love. Three years later, on September 12, 1758—after he had already entered into an understanding if not a formal en-gagement with his future wife, Martha Dandridge Custis— George wrote the now famous letter to Sally that included this passage:

> Tis true, I profess myself a Votary to Love—I acknowl-
> edge that a Lady is in the Case—and further I confess,

that this Lady is known to you—Yes Madam, as well as she is to one, who is too sensible of her Charms to deny the Power, whose Influence he feels and must ever Submit to. I feel the force of her amiable beauties in the recollection of a thousand tender passages that I could wish to obliterate, till I am bid to revive them—but experience alas! sadly reminds me how Impossible this is—and evinces an Opinion which I have long entertained, that there is a Destiny, which has the Sovereign control of our Actions—not to be resisted by the strongest efforts of Human Nature.

You have drawn me my dear Madam, or rather have I drawn myself, into an honest confession of a Simple Fact—misconstrue not my meaning—'tis obvious—doubt it not, nor expose it,—the World has no business to know the object of my Love, declared in this manner to you when I want to conceal it—One thing, above all things in this World I wish to know, and only one person of your Acquaintance can solve me that, or guess my meaning—but adieu to this, till happier times, if I ever shall see them.

The nature of the "thousand tender passages" besieging Washington's memory will always perplex historians, but there can be no doubting the earnestness of his letter, which Sally treasured until her death. And although there is no evidence that George ever cheated on Martha after they were married, the recollection of his relationship with Sally clearly held a special place in his heart. In 1785, during a visit to the ruins of Belvoir, which had been burned down during the war, George became so overcome with emotion at the memory of what he called "the happiest moments of my life" that he had to flee the scene. Sally, hearing of his behavior via her unwitting husband, broke down in tears.[8]

George Washington's marriage to Martha Dandridge Custis on January 6, 1759, was, like Sally Cary's marriage to George William Fairfax, initially a union of convenience. Martha, whose first husband had died in 1757, was the richest widow in Virginia—"the equivalent of a modern millionaire several times over."[9] George, though not so wealthy, was reasonably well-heeled, and the celebrity that he had achieved in wartime made him a rising star in Virginia politics and society. It was a good match for them both. To make matters even better, they fell in love. Martha, only twenty-eight at the time of their marriage, was an attractive if not ravishing young woman, smart and versed in the social graces, while George, a year her junior, still retained all the vigor and self-confidence of youth. And although they never had children, possibly because George had been sterilized by smallpox as a youth, their relationship was undoubtedly physical. As the years passed, they became ever more dependent on each other's company, so much so that Martha spent the majority of the Revolutionary War with her husband, even at places such as Valley Forge.

NATHANIEL HAWTHORNE NEED NOT have wondered: George Washington did take his clothes off, and quite often at that. Even his sense of humor reflected the bawdiness of his age. In 1786, joking about the mating of his prize jackass, Royal Gift, with a small and rather timid jenny, he wrote: "Though in appearance quite unequal to the match—yet, like a true female, she was not to be terrified at the disproportionate size of her paramour—& having renewed the conflict twice or thrice, it is to be hoped the issue will be favourable."[10] And in 1784, writing to his friend the Reverend William Gordon about the recent marriage of their mutual friend Joseph Ward at age forty-seven, Washington quipped: "Charity . . . induces me to suppose that like a prudent general, he had reviewed his *strength*, his arms, & ammunition before he got involved in an action—But if these have been neglected, & he has been precipitated into the measure, let me advise him to make the *first* onset upon his fair [lady], with vigor, that the impression may be deep, if it cannot be lasting, or frequently renewed."[11]

Eighteenth-century Americans were not generally as uncomfortable with the subject of sex as their descendants would become in subsequent generations. Among young men, especially members of the social elites, crude humor and sexual escapades were quite common. True, the usual double standard prevented women from taking the same liberties, although it did not restrict them as much as it would in the nineteenth century. The principles of decorum likewise forced morally suspect behavior to take shelter beneath a veneer of politesse and innuendo. On the whole, though, affairs out of wedlock—to say nothing of passionately physical marriages—were not considered outrageously shocking. If anything, Washington stood out among his contemporaries for the degree of his propriety and reserve—concepts foreign to Benjamin Franklin and Thomas Jefferson, among many others. Especially after he entered public life at the onset of the Revolutionary War, Washington grew obsessively careful about shielding himself from any suspicion of moral impropriety—not out of priggishness, but because he felt so profoundly the burden of maintaining his public image.

By the 1850s, Washington's charisma—indeed, his very physicality—had faded away to the point that his image became almost entirely asexual. Images of the Founder, generally modeled after the Gilbert Stuart painting of 1796, depicted him as a stiff and shriveled old man, betraying the merest hints of his youth. Moral standards, meanwhile, had changed. As necklines crept higher and hemlines lower, and the suffocating Victorian moral code took hold, so too did the human Washington recede until the very idea of his sexuality became shocking. His athleticism was a caricature, his marriage to Martha a mere matter of form. Even popular writers such as Mason Locke Weems avoided any hint of romance or passion in their retellings of the great man's life. In the public eye, Washington danced an eternal minuet, lifeless as a music box dancer.

Washington's emasculation, as with other elements of his dehumanization, frustrated average Americans—especially women. An elderly Founder identifiable only by his military and political feats, enveloped in a rigid, old-fashioned uniform, spoke little to their interests or the everyday concerns of their lives. The earliest attempts to revive his image in order to make him more appealing to women coincided with the discovery, in the mid-nineteenth century, of the female literary market. Shut out from traditionally masculine activities in the public sphere—with time on their hands, as it were— women had long been among the most avid American readers, but publishers did not recognize the profitability of literature directed to their tastes until around the mid-nineteenth century. Novels made up the bulk of the new feminine literature, but it quickly became apparent that women also wanted to read nonfiction, including history. How natural, then, to recast America's most popular historical figure, George Washington, for a female audience.

Caroline Matilda Kirkland wrote one of the first biographies of Washington marketed specifically for women. In her *Memoirs of Washington* (1857), she rediscovered her subject's youthful verve and displayed him in the full glory of his "manly" goodness and charm. Going straight against the grain of contemporary portraits, Kirkland outlined Washington's personal beauty and—scandal of scandals!—emphasized his "winning smile," which she claimed lit up his face. Instead of being stern and inscrutable, that face reflected modesty and tenderness of a sort that "might well become the countenance of a woman." Kirkland described the joy that he took in entertaining young ladies and the care with which he studied the "little matters that interested" women in order to make himself a more agreeable companion. Ladies dismissed his initially floundering juvenile efforts to impress them, but with maturity and the "hardening of his sinews," Kirkland slyly noted, he found very few who did not "prove kind." Further softening his image, she claimed that he adored romping with children. And when decorum forbade active play, he spied through cracks and keyholes on their games.

Kirkland's frothy anecdotes of Washington's love affairs were the feminine equivalents of George Lippard's boyish tales of blood and slaughter, and they had about as much to do with reality. Nevertheless, they recaptured a certain flavor of Washington's genuine youthful ardor. Jaded by war, Washington enters the "softening atmosphere" of Beverly Robinson's New York drawing room and immediately falls under the spell of the "handsome and sprightly" Mary Philipse. Overcome with passion, he fantasizes about plucking this "fair flower" and carrying her off to Mount Vernon. But alas! Another man, a wounded officer, indulges himself in the same dream, and trades successfully on his injury to win her affection. Shattered, Washington returns to Virginia, where another beauty, Martha Custis, holds his future in the palms of her pretty little hands. Kirkland's Martha is no dowdy frump but "a small, plump figure, full of sprightliness and feminine grace, fond of gayety, and not insensible to her many advantages; proud of her husband and making her duty to him the law of her life, yet loving her own way too, and claiming the privileges of her sex and circumstances." An engraving of the couple in Kirkland's book overturns other contemporary images by showing a fair yet manly Washington at table with a young and beautiful Martha, who fashionably sports ringlets and 1850s-style clothing.[12]

Kirkland especially would have enjoyed spinning tales out of Washington's "votary of love" letter to Sally Fairfax. At the time she wrote, however, its existence remained unknown. Still, absence of hard evidence never deterred idle gossip, and storytellers gleefully plied a fascinated public with fantastic tales of Washington's relationship with Sally and her sister Mary. Bishop William Meade, in his very popular book *Old Churches, Ministers and Families of Virginia* (1857), told how Washington asked for Mary's hand only to be rebuffed by her heartless father. "If that is your business here, sir," the old man raged, "I wish you to leave the house, for my daughter has been accustomed to ride in her own coach." Many years later, as Washington rode through Williamsburg at the head of his troops, poor Mary collapsed in a faint when her former lover spied her in the crowd and saluted her.[13] Other writers, including Washington Irving, retold these and other romantic stories but replaced Mary with Sally or another sister. An 1876 article in *Scribner's* claimed that Sally's niece, also named Sally, befriended Washington as a young girl, becoming his "Pet Marjorie." Some years later, age seventeen, she appeared at a ball. Her beauty overwhelmed Washington, by that time long married, enticing him to spend the evening dancing with her.[14]

Stories such as these were designed for entertainment rather than shock value. No one dared to hint at any lustiness or unfaithfulness that might have run contrary to Victorian moral codes. Even the publication of Washington's "votary of love" letter to Sally Fairfax in the *New York Herald* on March 30, 1877, did not at first cause much of a stir. On the following day an anonymous buyer purchased the letter at an auction for $13 and it disappeared, prompting some people to dismiss it as a fraud. About a decade later, however, writers "rediscovered" the letter in the context of a budding popular trend—inspired in part by the centennial of the first presidential inauguration—to humanize Washington by exposing his missteps and flaws.

Worthington Chauncey Ford printed the "votary of love" letter in 1889 in his fourteen-volume edition of *The Writings of Washington*. A careful scholar devoted to the preservation of historical manuscripts, Ford had no intention of creating controversy, but he also used the publication of the Fairfax letter as an occasion to examine references to the "lowland beauty" and other secret lovers. *Harper's* picked up on Ford's research in two articles, "Footprints in Washingtonland" and "Washington as Lover and Poet," in April and May 1889. Treating the "votary of love" letter as a bombshell that exposed an entirely new side of the first president, the articles dwelt at length on his supposed affair with Sally Fairfax. They also gave credence to an old rumor that a preteen Washington had been caught "romping with one of the largest girls" in his county, and indulged in meandering fantasies about the legions of female admirers who besieged him as a teen and young adult.

The *Harper's* articles and subsequent explorations of the first president's love life in the 1890s and early 1900s completely recast the gently romantic Washington popular in the 1850s. Kirkland's rose-garlanded Washington now appeared a little unsavory. Martha, meanwhile, flopped down into her corner rocking chair and grew old and fat. Writers reveled in her physical degeneration and supposed stupidity and ill temper, using it to justify her husband's infidelity. Moncure D. Conway, the author of "Footprints in Washingtonland," wrote that memories of the affair with Sally Fairfax consoled Washington through many loveless years with Martha, who had alienated him in part by her inability to bear him a daughter. Washington adored little girls, said Conway—without attempting to suggest any impropriety—and played with them at every opportunity. "The great athletic hardy soldier, bronzed and weather-beaten before he was thirty, loved to have these little dames nestling at his side."[15]

Newspapers across the country reprinted the *Harper's* stories numerous times over the following few years, solidifying the images of George the irrepressible lover and Martha the overweight hag. The lowland beauty, Mary Philipse, Sally Fairfax, and all of George's other young lovers simultaneously grew more fascinating. Paul Leicester Ford, Worthington Chauncey Ford's brother, published *The True George Washington* in 1896 with the professed aim of "humanizing

Washington, and making him a man rather than a historical figure." To this end, he dwelt endlessly on Washington's physique, social relations, daily amusements, and especially "relations with the fair sex." Paul Leicester Ford recounted slanderous old Tory rumors of Washington's kept woman, Mary Gibbons, and "Kate, the Washer-woman's daughter," both of whom supposedly slept with him on numerous occasions during the war. Ravishing beauties, gaily adorned and flashing wit and romance, twirl endlessly through the pages of Ford's book, stealing kisses and other favors from a hale and manly Washington—while Martha skulks toadlike in the shadows. "Over-fond, hot-tempered, obstinate, and a poor speller," she possessed, according to Ford, a certain type of merit as a "matronly and kind" sort of woman, but little more, and it is with an obvious sense of disappointment that he describes how Washington's marriage to her brought his sexual cavorting to a close.[16]

By the end of the 1890s and into the early 1900s, Washington the lover and dancer had almost completely supplanted "the rather abstract figure who once stood for national unity, moral rectitude, self-denial, and stoic devotion to duty."[17] Chalk one up for the humanizers, who had succeeded at least temporarily in spurring popular interest in the nation's Founder. Historian John Bach McMaster, in his eight-volume *History of the People of the United States*, celebrated this new focus as revealing "more of the man," and called on his peers to present the American people with more of the same. Future president Woodrow Wilson happily obliged in an 1896 biography of Washington that oozed "vaporous" and almost entirely spurious tales of romantic dalliances, replete with ornate illustrations by Howard Pyle. Wilson's political enemy Henry

Cabot Lodge gleefully joined in the silliness. "How much this little interlude . . . tells of the real man!" he exclaimed. "How the statuesque myth and the priggish myth and the dull and solemn myth melt away before it!"[18]

The stories grew more imaginative—or ridiculous—with each passing year. Thomas Allen Glenn, in *Some Colonial Mansions and Those Who Lived in Them* (1900), concocted a new and improved version of the Philipse romance:

> One version of this historic love-affair tells how they sat together in conversation until daybreak, and, as the gray light of morning crept in, mocking the flickering light of the candles burning low in their sockets, Washington at last found courage to propose, only to be refused. The story continues that the handsome young Virginian colonel grew ashy pale—which is the proper thing, by the way, to do under such circumstances—and rushed out of the house, upsetting one of the slaves who was up getting breakfast.[19]

General Bradley Johnson, writing in 1897 with appropriately military masculinity, imagined the "hundred other girls from Boston to Annapolis with whom the young Virginia colonel flirted and made love," and claimed that he "fell in love with every pretty girl and told her so." This, Johnson boasted, showed that Washington was "a man all over, a man with strong appetites, . . . positive, belligerent, and aggressive."[20] Valerie Hope, writing in the *Belleville News Democrat* in 1908 on "The Love Affairs of George Washington," told of a young Washington "pining and sighing and grating his teeth in despair" as an endless series of lovers enticed his passion and then heedlessly threw him over. "Washington was too wise to turn into a woman hater merely because he had been thrown down three times in succession," she wrote; however, "he knew there were plenty of pretty fish in the aquarium and that it would only be a matter of time when he'd make a good catch."[21] By 1900, boy guides at Alexandria, Virginia, were repeating stories of Washington meeting Sally Fairfax at a ball after his marriage to Martha: "He was comin' down stairs with Miss Sally Fairfax and they wuz gone on each other, and Miss Sally she got mad because George made goo-goo eyes at Mrs. Custis."[22]

Such gossip did offend some people—but not because of its inaccuracy. Instead, they raged at how it submerged Washington in a swamp of wickedness and perversion. Writing in 1903, Edward C. Towne decried misguided attempts "to apply a method of detraction to the character of Washington, and to reduce his greatness to the common level, upon the theory that we gain a man while we lose a hero." Worthington Chauncey Ford's edition of Washington's writings, he claimed, had been "executed on lines deliberately and avowedly intended to bring Washington down from his high historic pedestal," and his brother Paul Leicester Ford had attempted to reduce Washington to a "common historic character."[23] Leonard Irving, writing in the *Magazine of American History*, denounced the "sneers" and gossip-mongering that increasingly passed for reasoned historical analysis, and fretted at allegations that Washington actually cursed. Such rare oaths as he occasionally uttered, insisted Irving, were manifestations of Washington's "vigorous manhood" rather than evidence of a degraded character.[24]

Towne and Irving hadn't seen anything yet. In the teens

and twenties, writers churned out dozens of popular biographies such as *Sally Cary: A Long Hidden Romance of Washington's Life* (1916), *George Washington as Housekeeper with Glimpses of His Domestic Arrangements, Dining, Company, Etc.* (1924), and *The Family Life of George Washington* (1926), all of them swooning over Washington's romantic antics. Then the debunkers got to work. Furious at the Victorian-era deification of America's Founders, the debunkers hacked the classical image of Washington to pieces, replacing it with a foulmouthed, whiskey-swilling, tobacco-chomping ignoramus who ruined more virgins than any man in Virginia. In 1926, an article in *Scribner's* cited a story suggesting that Washington's death had resulted from a cold caught while riding to an "assignation with an overseer's wife." Eugene E. Prussing wrote another article in the same periodical claiming that Martha had burned her correspondence with her husband in order to cover up their lack of affection, and might even have burned George's letters to his many lovers. John Pierpont Morgan's private librarian claimed that his boss had sought out and destroyed a number of "smutty" Washington letters for the same purpose. Others claimed that cryptic marks in his diary recorded sexual liaisons, and that he had hidden one or more illegitimate children.[25]

W. E. Woodward and Rupert Hughes—the grand dukes of debunkery—repeated these stories and many more in biographies published in 1926. Woodward, the more cynical of the two, painted Washington as an "intensely masculine" but otherwise awkward fumbler who adored women but never quite figured them out. Deformed by grotesquely large hands and feet, he pawed apelike at every girl who passed his way, only to suffer through one jilt after another. At first Washington recoiled into "mooning and moping," but before long he found an opportunity to take his revenge on womankind. One day in the summer of 1750, while Washington bathed in the Rappahannock River, two servant girls ran off with his clothes. Woodward reveled in the ensuing scene:

> Only fancy! The Father of Our Country standing by the river's brink in the golden sunset clad only in humorless dignity—for, although he had plenty of dignity he never had any humor—clothed in dignity, and wondering how to get home. Eventually he got home somehow, and had the girls arrested. One of them was convicted of theft and was punished with fifteen lashes on her bare back.

The episode did indeed take place—the records of it are in the Spotsylvania County courthouse—but it revealed nothing about Washington's feelings toward women or his supposed lack of a sense of humor. Hughes took a more upbeat approach by comparing Washington's antics with those of the contemporary smart set. His Washington seemed less at home in a grand ballroom than in a speakeasy with flappers hanging on his arms.[26]

Patriotic organizations and conservative periodicals denounced the debunkers, but with little effect. People called them self-righteous prudes. As the Roaring Twenties faded and the Great Depression and World War II gripped the headlines, however, Americans lost patience with the debunkers' increasingly outrageous attempts to debase their national icons. In *The George Washington Scandals* (1929), John C. Fitzpatrick—future editor of the monumental thirty-seven-volume *Writings of Washington*—booted the debunkers out the window, tracing their madcap tales back to Tory lies or, in many cases, thin air. Hughes, Woodward, and all the others amounted in Fitzpatrick's eyes to "ignorant scandalmongers" addicted to a culture of "twittering sensationalism."[27] Scholars also called for an end to the scurrilous gossip. Douglas Southall Freeman and Marcus Cunliffe, writing in the 1940s and 1950s, dismissed the "votary of love" letter, which appeared to have started the whole mess, as a rank forgery. By the time the original letter reappeared, in 1958 in Harvard's Houghton Library, the brouhaha had ended. Interest in Washington's domestic and social life did not disappear, of course, but mid-twentieth-century writers either toned down their tales of romance or presented them straight out as fiction.

The debunkers never quite left the scene. Historian James Thomas Flexner, author of the extremely popular four-volume biography *George Washington* (1965–72), resurrected the image of Martha as an overfed shrew and imagined her husband overwhelmed with passion for Sally Fairfax. And near the end of the century, as will be discussed later, revelations of Thomas Jefferson's affair with Sally Hemings led some to accuse Washington of fathering a child, West Ford, by a slave named Venus. For the most part, though, chroniclers of Washington's sexual career have been content to recycle older and relatively pedestrian fantasies originating in the nineteenth century.

More usefully, some historians have undertaken the long-overdue task of rescuing Martha Washington from the stereotypes to which generations of hagiographers and debunkers alike had consigned her. Suggestions that Martha was ugly and disagreeable and that her marriage with George lacked affection have been proven inaccurate. To the contrary, a good deal of evidence exists to show that she was beautiful, witty, and intelligent, and that she and her husband loved each other deeply. Here, too, however, the human capacity for self-delusion has peeped through the scholarship. A computerized age-regression portrait of Martha composed in 2006 by a team of forensic anthropologists under the guidance of historian Patricia Brady—though far more true to life than any previous attempt to render her as a young woman—oozes sexuality and might easily adorn the cover of a bodice-ripping romance novel. Enraptured journalists responded by exclaiming that "Martha Washington was *hot*" and that her famous second husband was a "hunk."[28] Likewise, attempts to demonstrate her active participation in George Washington's life at times make her resemble a modern feminist lording it over a somewhat dim-witted and obsequious husband rather than the attractive, smart, but largely conventional woman that she in fact was. In the end, Martha is simply being remolded to suit the interests and desires of a new generation. Her husband would certainly understand.

CHAPTER 4

Washington's Visions

STAN HENKELS ADMIRED George Washington, and he hated forgeries. His decades of experience as a Philadelphia bookseller and auctioneer had inured him to all the tricks of the trade, and con men found him almost impossible to fool. Collectors regarded him as one of the most trustworthy dealers in America. Only two types of people unsettled him: liars and Yankees. An unreconstructed Confederate who pined for the days of Jeff Davis and the Stars and Bars, Henkels lost his cool at any mention of Dixie. His regular customers quickly learned how to take advantage of this idiosyncrasy. "An appeal to his Southern patriotism," said one, "was the only thing that could unsettle his judgment."[1]

Washington had been good to Henkels. As the popularity of Washington memorabilia grew in the wake of the Centennial of 1876, Henkels earned a healthy profit by specializing in

Founding-era books and manuscripts, especially those relating to the life of the country's first president. In the process, he uncovered and denounced numerous forgeries by Robert Spring and others, thus increasing his reputation for reliability. On February 11, 1891, Henkels opened what he marketed as perhaps the most important auction of the century. This auction of "Washingtonian and rare American literary and historical curiosities" included dozens of items in a collection descending directly from Washington's own family. The biggest names in book and manuscript collecting attended or sent representatives, as did the New York, Boston, Chicago, and Richmond libraries. Reporters from the major newspapers also thronged the opening, and Henkels proudly told one that he had personally sold "almost everything of value relating to our first President" but that this collection, which he would dispose of in a series of auctions, contained "the most interesting, valuable, and truly historical documents" of any that he had ever seen. Lots going under the hammer included a catalog of the library at Mount Vernon, Washington's own copy of the Philadelphia city directory, his personal world atlas, a book belonging to and signed by his mother, a lock of his hair, the silver plate from his coffin, and numerous signed manuscripts. "The prices realized," said a reporter from the *New York Times*, "were far beyond expectation and altogether unprecedented."[2]

Two months later, Henkels opened another auction consisting of items from the same collection from the Washington family. This time the lots included an item altogether novel and unprecedented: "Gen'l Geo. Washington's Manuscript Prayer Book, entitled the 'Daily Sacrifice.'" Henkels described it thus in his catalog: "This gem is all in the handwriting of Geo. Washington, when about twenty years old, and is, without exception, the most hallowed of all his writings. It is neatly written on twenty-four pages of a little book about the size of the ordinary pocket memorandum." There followed a lengthy quote from the prayer book, including the following passage from the prayer for Sunday morning:

> Let my heart, therefore, gracious God, be so affected with the glory and majesty of it, that I may not do mine own works but wait on thee, and discharge those weighty duties, thou requires of me; and since thou are a God of pure eyes, and wilt be sanctified in all who draw near unto thee, who dost not regard the sacrifice of fools, nor hear sinners who tread in thy courts, pardon I beseech thee, my sins, remove them from thy presence, as far as the east is from the west; and accept of me for the merits of thy Son Jesus Christ, that when I come into thy temple, and compass thine Altar, my prayer may come before thee as incense, and as I desire thou wouldst hear me calling upon thee in my prayers, so give me grace to hear thee calling on me in thy word, that it may be wisdom, righteousness, reconciliation, and peace to the saving of my soul on the day of the Lord Jesus.[3]

Henkels told an interesting story about the document's origins. While sorting through the vast collection of items that he had received from the Washington family—its provenance went all the way back to Bushrod Washington, who had inherited it from George Washington—Henkels had discovered a dilapidated old trunk filled with miscellaneous papers. The owner of the collection told him not to bother with the trunk. Representatives of the Smithsonian Institution had already perused the contents and rejected them as worthless. But Henkels, like any good dealer, persisted and came upon the prayer book. Its contents, he decided after consulting anonymous "experts," were undoubtedly in Washington's early handwriting. He sold it as genuine, for $1,250.[4]

Henkels, an honest but fallible man, had been hoodwinked. More accurately, he had hoodwinked himself. The Washington prayer book was a fake. Though incomplete (it ended abruptly in the middle of the prayer for Thursday morning) and unsigned, it had been penned in handwriting obviously intended to resemble Washington's. That it did—just barely—but in writing far more crude than anything Washington had written as an adult. Henkels explained this away by claiming that Washington must have composed the prayer book as a young man. But the argument could not hold up, as anyone with access to Washington's genuine youthful writings could have discovered at a glance. Compared side by side, there is no resemblance whatsoever.[5]

Critics immediately challenged the prayer book's authenticity and waged a running debate for weeks in the columns of the *New York Evening Post*. But some respected scholars came to Henkels's defense. Professors Lyman Abbott and S. F. Upham—Yankees both, but Henkels took allies wherever he could find them—hailed the prayer book as evidence of "that source of strength which sustained [Washington] with a divinely-inspired patience in an epoch in which mere enthusiasm of humanity, unnourished by secret springs of piety, must have dried up and utterly failed." The prayer book's purchaser, the Reverend Dr. Charles F. Hoffman, vice chancellor of Hobart College, defiantly proclaimed that it contained a "sermon every page" and that he was considering dividing it up for deposit in the fireproof vaults of college libraries across the nation, while making complete copies available for the edification of young men. The critics eventually quieted down, and the triumphant proponents of Washington the Christian took possession of the field.[6]

Secularist debunkers took on the prayer book in the 1920s and slammed it as a fake. Their arguments were irrefutable, and mainstream academics and journalists subsequently shied away from mentioning it. But the prayer book did not go away. Reprinted, most notably in Herbert Burk's *Washington's Prayers* (1907), it gained widespread credence in evangelical Christian circles, and remains popular in some quarters even today. The website of Pat Robertson's Christian Broadcasting Network, CBN.com, reproduces the entire text of the prayer journal. Author Tim LaHaye, a favorite of many evangelicals, wrote in 1990 that the prayer book proved that Washington would "freely identify with the Bible-believing branch of evangelical Christianity that is having such a positive influence on our nation." Televangelist James Kennedy used it to justify his belief that Washington "came to trust in the shed blood of Christ, the perfect life of Jesus Christ, in which he was robed and in which he stood before God." And Washington impersonator James Manship, who appears frequently at state and U.S. government functions and prays in uniform with children at Scouting events and in schools, campaigns tirelessly to convince people that the prayer book is an authentic document. Washington, he claims, was no deist, but a "prayer warrior."[7]

*   *   *

GEORGE WASHINGTON, A MAN of strong inner emotions, never spoke openly about his faith—or lack thereof. Just why is unclear. Maybe he considered professions of religious partisanship to be inconsistent with his sense of public decorum. Or perhaps, deep down, he just wasn't very interested in religion. Of his interest in philosophy there can be no doubt. An admirer of classical virtues, he lived according to a Stoic code. Providence—he generally preferred that word over direct references to God—was Washington's all-governing power. Each man, he believed, must walk the path that Providence laid out for him, serving the public good to the best of his abilities, and accepting trials and responsibilities without murmur.

Washington considered attendance at religious services to be a civic duty. He believed that morality and the unfettered practice of religion ensured the prosperity of a well-organized society. Beyond that, each man's conscience—including Washington's—was his own affair. Nominally an Episcopalian, he attended many religious services of different denominations, but he showed passion for none. Nor is there any firm evidence—despite some secularists' claims—that he preferred the popular elite "religion" of his day, deism, although he borrowed some of its language. He was a devoted Freemason, but even that dovetailed with his conception of civic duty. Few public figures in the United States or Europe could move up in society during the eighteenth century without belonging to the Masonic fraternity.

Was Washington a Christian? If anyone asked him, he might well have said yes. He was familiar with the Bible and even quoted it on occasion. But did he truly *believe*? That is an entirely different matter. Intelligent arguments can and have been made on both sides of the subject. Ultimately, however, they all come down to speculation. Thanks in large part to Washington's own efforts—he concealed his inner feelings from everyone, except perhaps Martha—we can never really know exactly what he did or did not believe about God. Alas, this truth remains unsatisfying. Americans have never really accepted it and probably never will.

Immediately after Washington's death, clerical eulogists made exaggerated claims, unsupported by evidence, of his Christianity. In the years that followed, writers and orators built up an edifice of Washingtonian piety, adapting it to their own preferences and needs. A typical example was Episcopal bishop William Meade's influential *Old Churches, Ministers and Families of Virginia* (1857), which transformed Washington into a puritanical zealot. Mistaking Washington's stoically inspired belief in decorum and restraint for fanaticism, Meade decided that the Founder had no tolerance for swearing, drinking, gambling, hunting, theater, or even dancing.[8]

Meanwhile, the image of "Washington discovered in prayer" spread through popular folklore. Almost every day of his life, it seemed, someone had rounded a corner, opened a door, or parted bushes to discover Washington in prayer; so much so that one wonders if he ever got a moment to himself. In time, "truth" became established through simple repetition. In 1884, the Reverend Philip Slaughter stood before the Mount Vernon Ladies' Association and complacently assured his audience that Washington spent two hours each day praying and reading the Bible and that "confessions of faith" appeared in "nearly every public document issued by him from the beginning to the close of his career, as soldier and states-man."[9] By the end of the nineteenth century, most Americans took Washington's Christian piety for granted.

The prayer book is the most obvious but by no means the only pious fake to enter the popular culture. Nineteenth-century Americans, inventive and industrious in so many re-spects, excelled at concocting false Washington quotations. Many of these quotations addressed religion. One of the most enduringly popular has Washington stating that "it is impos-sible to rightly govern the world without God and the Bible." Variously worded, this phrase has been repeated endlessly in books, speeches, and now on the Internet. For a time, Repub-lican leader Newt Gingrich advertised it on his website as an excerpt from Washington's "personal journal," and conserva-tive commentator Sean Hannity read it to raucous applause at a Values Voters Summit in September 2008, claiming that it came from the Founder's Farewell Address. Glenn Beck repeated it on his Fox television show on March 5, 2010. But the quote is bogus. Most likely originating in the nineteenth century, it has been debunked a thousand times over.[10]

Another popular quote, often called "Washington's Prayer," reads:

Almighty God, we make our earnest prayer that thou wilt keep these United States in thy holy protection, that thou wilt incline the hearts of the citizens to cultivate a spirit of subordination and obedience to government; to entertain a brotherly affection and love for one another and for their fellow citizens of the United States at large, and finally that thou wilt most graciously be pleased to

dispose us all to do justice, to love mercy and to demean
ourselves with that charity, humility and pacific temper of
mind which were the characteristics of the Divine Author
of our blessed religion, and without an humble imitation
of Whose example in these things we can never hope to
be a happy nation. Grant our supplication, we beseech
thee, through Jesus Christ our Lord. Amen.

These words, which are engraved on a bronze tablet in St.
Paul's Chapel in New York City, derive from an actual letter:
Washington's circular letter to the states of June 8, 1783, in
which he announced his intention to resign as commander
in chief of the army after the war's official conclusion. But
they have been cleverly modified. In the original, Washington
wrote:

I now make it my earnest prayer, that God would have
you, and the State over which you preside, in his holy
protection, that he would incline the hearts of the Citizens to cultivate a spirit of subordination and obedience to Government, to entertain a brotherly affection
and love for one another, for their fellow Citizens of the
United States at large, and particularly for their brethren
who have served in the Field, and finally, that he would
most graciously be pleased to dispose us all, to do Justice,
to love mercy, and to demean ourselves with that Charity, humility and pacific temper of mind, which were
the Characteristicks of the Divine Author of our blessed
Religion, and without an humble imitation of whose example in these things, we can never hope to be a happy
Nation.[11]

This letter provides some evidence of Washington's belief in God—but it did not suffice for some anonymous person, who reworded it as a prayer. At the February 2007 National Prayer Breakfast, attended by President George W. Bush and Senators Hillary Clinton, John McCain, and Barack Obama, among others, this "prayer" was quoted verbatim. It has also been quoted on innumerable occasions in speeches on the House and Senate floor.[12]

Religious folklore has so permeated the literature on Washington that it becomes difficult to distinguish fact from fiction. In my book *General George Washington: A Military Life* (2005), I used a secondary source to describe Washington's first appearance before the Continental army at Cambridge, Massachusetts, in July 1775. That source cited a nineteenth-century local history book that claimed Washington read his troops a passage from the 101st Psalm. I described the alleged scene without bothering to check its source. After my book's publication (it always happens that way), an alert blogger named J. L. Bell called me out. Washington, he determined, had probably never read the 101st Psalm to his troops. Instead, the story had probably originated in an article printed in an abolitionist newspaper in 1846, recounting tales told by an aged Revolutionary War veteran who actually had been nowhere near Cambridge in 1775. Since then, the story had been retold by Harriet Beecher Stowe, among others. Bell also dug up another Victorian legend about Washington and the 101st Psalm—this time suggesting that British admiral Lord Richard Howe had sent the psalm to Washington in order to inspire him to endure the war's dark days—and demonstrated how subsequent historians had misused it.[13]

Another widely beloved religious myth concerns the

alleged full-immersion baptism of Washington by the Reverend John Gano, a Baptist minister from New York who served as a military chaplain during the war. In the 1870s and 1880s, some of Gano's descendants signed curious affidavits asserting that he had privately baptized Washington by full immersion during the winter at Valley Forge. They provided no description—though it would have been a very colorful one—of Washington trudging through mud and slush down to the rain-swollen and ice-choked Schuylkill River, enduring a frigid dunking at Gano's hands, and then scampering back to headquarters to frantically rub his frozen bottom in front of the fire. Instead, they said that Washington not unreasonably wished the affair to be kept private.

The baptism legend seems to have circulated by word of mouth until 1908, when a minister at a Manhattan church commissioned an artist to paint a portrait of Gano and Washington sloshing about in the Potomac (not the Schuylkill) River. The painting hung in a Baptist church in Asbury Park, New Jersey, until 1926, when Gano's great-granddaughter donated it to the Baptist William Jewell College in Liberty, Missouri. She required the college to hang it in a chapel to be named after Gano and built with her funds. Although the college did and does not take any stance on the legend's authenticity, others have attempted to lend it credence. In 1926, the *Bulletin of William Jewell College* published an article purporting to show Gano's "intimate" relationship with Washington—in fact, Washington never mentions Gano in his diaries or correspondence, and there is no record that the two ever met—and demonstrate the reliability of the baptism legend.

After further elaborations on the story in various minor articles and pamphlets, a Sigma Nu fraternity newspaper caught the mainstream press's eye by claiming that Washington had told Gano: "I have been investigating the Scripture, and I believe immersion to be baptism taught in the Word of God, and I demand it at your hands. I do not wish any parade made or the army called out, but simply a quiet demonstration of the ordinance." According to this revised version, Gano then baptized Washington (who had already been sprinkled as an infant) in the Potomac in front of forty-two witnesses— none of whom ever surfaced. *Time* magazine summarized the fraternity paper's story in its September 5, 1932, issue, and although historians immediately rejected the tale, it gained popular traction. Charles W. Koller, president of the Northern Baptist Theological Seminary, spread the word in Baptist newsletters and magazines after World War II, transferring the scene to the Hudson River, and although many Baptists recognized it as a fraud, it still pops up in the occasional sermon.[14]

IT IS NO COINCIDENCE that the earliest versions of the Gano legend placed the dunking at Valley Forge. Storytellers have always had a particular fixation with the terrible winter encampment of 1777–78. Perhaps it is because the Continental army's survival through that difficult time seems nothing short of miraculous. Certainly the patriotic lexicon has made it seem so. The foremost of the Valley Forge legends is that of Washington kneeling in the snow and supplicating God for deliverance. President Ronald Reagan, speaking on May 6, 1982, declared that "the most sublime picture in American history is of George Washington on his knees in the snow at Valley Forge."[15] From this trunk, many elaborate branches have grown.

The story of Washington's prayer at Valley Forge appeared for the first time in an article that Mason Locke Weems wrote for *The Federalist* in 1804. He then reprinted it in the 1817 edition of his *Life of Washington*.[16] Weems's source for the story is unknown; it may have been a piece of popular folklore that he heard orally, or it could have emerged from his imagination. Not long after its publication, however, Presbyterian minister Nathaniel Randolph Snowden wrote in his unpublished remembrances that he had received the story directly from the Quaker who had discovered Washington in prayer and converted to the revolutionary cause. But his version and Weems's did not agree. Weems named the Quaker as Isaac Potts, who owned the house in which the commander in chief established his headquarters, and called his wife Sarah. Snowden, by contrast, identified the eavesdropper as John Potts, presumably having confused Isaac with his father, John senior, who died in 1768, or his brother John junior, an unrepentant Tory who had fled to Nova Scotia. But it couldn't have been Isaac, either, for he did not live anywhere near Valley Forge at the time—he had rented out his home to his aunt—and he did not marry his wife, Sarah, until 1803.[17]

The prayer story's dubious origins did not dissuade others from repeating it as fact. Most simply took Weems's version and modified it to suit their tastes. Dozens of newspapers repeated the story, without reference to its origins, during Lafayette's visit to the United States in 1824–25. In 1836, the Reverend Edward C. M'Guire wrote a book about Washington's religious beliefs, in which he reprinted a story that a Baptist minister had sent to a newspaper some years before. Washington had often gone to pray in a grove at Valley Forge, the minister claimed, and had been detected there by one Devault Beaver and no less a figure than General Henry Knox. To this M'Guire appended other stories of Washington discovered in prayer.[18] Benson J. Lossing, in his popular and oft-reprinted *Pictorial Field-Book of the Revolution* (1852), retold it with new details, such as that Washington had tied his horse to a sapling nearby and that his face had been "suffused with tears."[19] In 1878, a New York periodical called the *Aldine Press* printed a tale of Lafayette and General Peter Muhlenberg discovering Washington in prayer at Valley Forge on some hay strewn about the floor of a barn. Countless other writers repeated the legend—including, as mentioned earlier, George Lippard—but without mentioning Weems or Snowden as their source.[20]

Other "prayer stories" became popular, too. In 1895, the *New York Times* claimed that Washington, stressed out from a series of defeats in the autumn of 1776 and preparing to lead his troops into battle at White Plains, New York, spontaneously and publicly blurted out a prayer from the Book of Joshua: "The Lord God of gods, the Lord God of gods, he knoweth, and Israel he shall know; if it be in rebellion, or if in transgression against the Lord, save us not this day." "To his mind," the newspaper suggested, "his mission as the leader for the struggle for freedom was akin to that of Joshua and the children of Israel."[21] Stories circulated around the same time that someone had heard Washington groaning God's name from the depths of a thorny thicket near Princeton—not, presumably, because he found it difficult to free himself from the brambles but because he feared for the fate of his army. Storytellers also claimed—borrowing an allusion made back in 1859 by George Washington Parke Custis—that he adopted the habit of rising to say a blessing before every meal. Another tale, told in all seriousness, claimed that General Nathanael Greene had once dared to interrupt the commander in chief's private devotions only to scamper away in fear after Washington rose, fired a pistol at his unwelcome guest, and returned placidly to his prayers.[22]

More recently, Chuck Colson—a former special counsel to President Richard Nixon who spent time in prison after Watergate and subsequently established a Christian prison ministry—ran a radio commentary titled "Why Washington is 'The Father of Our Country.'" In it, he repeated the tale of a Quaker finding Washington at prayer in the snow, and insisted that the Founder was "a man of profound Christian piety." CBN, which propagates the alleged "prayer journal," also has the entire transcript of Colson's broadcast online. The conservative Family Research Council, chronicling the evening before Washington's famous crossing of the Delaware River on Christmas Day, 1776, claimed on its website: "We have no record of Washington's prayer that Christmas Eve, but we know he prayed. It was his habit to rise early every morning to spend an hour in prayer and reflection on the Word and to spend yet another hour in prayer each evening before putting his head to the pillow."[23]

The image of Washington in prayer became iconic. Lambert Sachs painted it in 1854, showing Washington on his knees in a gesture of supplication while an eavesdropper lurks in the wooded background, but without any snow. Henry Brueckner painted the best-known picture of the prayer in 1866, complete with snow and a few soldiers huddling over a fire in the background. Engraved and distributed widely in books and newspapers, Brueckner's version became a popular decoration in thousands of American households.

The U.S. Postal Service printed the Brueckner engraving on a 2-cent stamp in 1928 to commemorate the 150th anniversary of the Valley Forge encampment. Artist J. C. Leyendecker painted another popular rendition of the prayer for the cover of the February 23, 1935, *Saturday Evening Post*, and it appeared again on a 13-cent Christmas stamp in 1977. Arnold Friberg painted the best-known modern version of the image in 1976 to commemorate the Bicentennial. All of these images incorporate Lossing's invention—the horse tied nearby, which did not feature in Weems's or Snowden's versions—and make Washington look about twenty years older than he was at the time.[24]

From paintings and engravings, the prayer image spread across the country in a multitude of forms. On February 22, 1907, a bronze tablet depicting the commander in chief praying in the snow at Valley Forge was unveiled at the Sub-Treasury Building (now Federal Hall) at Broad and Nassau Streets in New York City. It had been modeled after a tablet by prominent sculptor J. E. Kelly that adorned the YMCA building in the same city. Kelly, who prided himself on his realism, had undertaken the job of depicting the prayer only after conducting research that left him "fully convinced of its historic basis and authenticity on all points." No one questioned him, but the Treasury Department objected to initial plans to place the donor's name at the base of the replica on the Sub-Treasury Building. The name was quickly removed, but another objection arose as someone noted a regulation preventing Treasury Department buildings from displaying copies of original artwork. With creditable persistence, the tablet's sponsors simply swapped the copy with the original at the YMCA, and the Washington Colonial Guards, various military detachments, and veterans' organizations, along with the Hebrew Orphan Asylum, celebrated the unveiling in due course. The only objection came from "A. Hoosier," who wrote to the *New York Times* begging someone to remove the "bronze nightmare" from the Sub-Treasury Building and send it far away. "Couldn't the President present it to the German Emperor?" he asked. "If he was hypnotized he would accept it. Help us out. The thing is getting on our nerves."[25]

Unfazed by such sarcasm, Washington's prayer warriors proudly carried their totem onward to new battlefields. In 1903, the George Washington Memorial Chapel was founded at Valley Forge with a stained-glass window depicting the commander in chief at prayer. Fifteen years later, someone offered to erect a statue at the nearby military park, only to be rebuffed after the chief of the manuscript division at the Library of Congress told the park authorities, "If the prayer story can ever be authenticated, there could be no possible objection to a marker on the spot, but . . . it cheapens Valley Forge, and tends to destroy the atmosphere of the place when mere tradition is monumented with all the solemnity of established fact." But in 1967, the Pennsylvania Freemasons gave the Freedoms Foundation at Valley Forge a massive nine-foot statue of a kneeling Washington to be placed at the entrance to the foundation's Congressional Medal of Honor Grove. Wilber M. Brucker, former secretary of the army, spoke at the monument's dedication and expressed his hope that it would inspire Americans to stay the course in Vietnam. Washington "didn't cringe during eight long years of warfare," he said. "Instead of listening to impatient counsel of defeat, America should tighten its belt and resolutely turn again to the grim task of destroying Communist aggression."[26] And in Washington, D.C., the U.S. Capitol's Congressional Prayer Room was founded in 1955 with a stained-glass window depicting Washington praying the 16th Psalm surrounded by the Great Seal of the United States and the names of the fifty states. Placed with government sanction at such important locations, who could doubt that Washington had knelt down and prayed in the snow at Valley Forge?

THE REVEREND NATHANIEL SNOWDEN's unpublished memoirs, which lent credence to the Valley Forge prayer story, also repeated a legend claiming that Washington took communion at a public service during the 1779–80 winter encampment at Morristown, New Jersey. "When the army lay at Morristown," Snowden wrote, "the Rev. Dr. Jones, administered the sacrament of ye Lord's supper. Washington came forward at ye head of all his officers and took his seat at ye 1st table, & took of ye bread and wine, the Symbols of Christ's broken body and shed blood, to do this in remembrance of ye L[ord] J[esus] C[hrist] & thus professed himself a Christian & a disciple of the blessed Jesus."[27]

This legend, which has also proved enduringly popular, first appeared in the appendix to David Hosack's *Memoir of DeWitt Clinton*, published in 1829. Hosack, best known as the doctor who tended to Alexander Hamilton after his duel with Aaron Burr in 1804, had by the 1820s overcome early associations with grave robbers to become one of the most prominent physicians and scientists in the United States. Hosack's many friends included the Reverend Samuel Hanson Cox, a Presbyterian minister at the Laight Street Church in New York City and a prominent abolitionist. Cox wrote to Hosack on March 20, 1828, with a curious story that he had picked up from "unquestionable authority," namely, an anonymous "venerable clergyman." Over three decades earlier, Cox informed his friend, another elderly preacher named Timothy Johnes had told the unnamed clergyman that he had administered communion to Washington during an outdoor service at the Morristown Presbyterian Church.

The tale went as follows. One morning, Washington had just finished inspecting his camp when he dropped by the Reverend Dr. Johnes's home near Morristown. "Doctor," the general said, "I understand that the Lord's Supper is to be celebrated with you next Sunday; I would learn if it accords with the canons of your church to admit communicants of another denomination?" "Most certainly," Johnes replied; "ours is not the Presbyterian table, General, but the Lord's table; and we hence give the Lord's invitation to all his followers, of whatever name." Pleased at this display of ecumenical piety, Washington responded that he was "glad of it; that is as it ought to be: but as I was not quite sure of the fact, I thought I would ascertain it from yourself, as I propose to join with you on that occasion. Though a member of the Church of England, I have no exclusive partialities." And there he was the following Sunday, following through the entire service and gravely receiving communion.

As typical with stories of this sort, it changed over time. Snowden treated it as a public and deliberate affirmation of Christian faith. Others claimed that Washington returned "often" to hear the Gospel, and romantically elaborated the tale with accounts of a church building full of wounded soldiers, an apple tree towering over the altar, and Washington giving up his chair to a young woman with a child.[28] Images of the service grew popular, and a painting of it was hung in Philadelphia's Presbyterian Hospital.[29] Proof that it had ever happened, however, remained elusive. In 1836, a woman went to visit Johnes's surviving family members and asked them what they knew of the tale. None of them could remember hearing it from the minister himself, and his son, though still alive, had grown senile. The son's wife also had never heard the story from the minister, but called it an "unquestioned family tradition." Persisting, the woman quizzed every old family member she could find in the Morristown area. Surely someone had seen the event, or at least knew someone who had seen it? No—although, she stubbornly concluded, "it is believed there are such."[30]

Washington's communion at Johnes's service certainly would have excited remark, especially as he had scrupulously avoided the sacrament at his own Episcopal church in Alexandria. Yet no one, including Johnes or any of Washington's officers, ever testified to this alleged very public event except for Snowden, who would have been nineteen or twenty years old at the time. Nor did Washington mention Johnes or taking communion in any of his correspondence for this period. So while it is *possible* that someone discovered Washington in prayer at Valley Forge—just as it is *possible* (though admittedly less plausible) that someone found him hopping about in his underwear and singing "God Save the King"—it remains extremely unlikely, especially given Washington's well-known refusal to kneel in church. Nor have any other eyewitness accounts of Washington in prayer ever emerged, which is peculiar given claims that he did so every day.

* * *

NOT ALL OF THE RELIGIOUS TRADITIONS of Washington at Valley Forge are Christian. In the 1880s and 1890s, some books claimed that Washington had visited one Daniel Hart, a Jew living in Philadelphia. The visit probably never took place—there is no primary evidence for it—but in this simple form the story amounted to just another of the relatively harmless "George Washington slept here" stories common in local folklore. But it did not end there. Sometime in the twentieth century stories circulated—probably orally—that Washington had told Hart of an episode at Valley Forge on the evening of Christmas Day, 1777. Entering a shack where some soldiers had bedded down, the story goes, Washington noticed a young soldier off in a corner, softly crying. The general asked the lad what troubled him, and noticed that he held a strange lamp. The soldier replied that it was his Hanukkah lamp and that he was a Jew recently arrived from Poland. He then told Washington about how the lamp commemorated the victory of a small band of Israelites over a much larger foe, and explained that he had cried in hopes that the Continental army would experience the same kind of victory. The experience, Washington allegedly told Hart, inspired him to fight on against all odds. Taking hold among the Jewish American immigrant community, the legend spread and appeared in several books— most recently Stephen Krensky's award-winning children's book, *Hanukkah at Valley Forge* (2006). The story, says Krensky, "is based on facts, but the tale itself must be taken on faith."[31]

*   *   *

OF ALL THE RELIGIOUS LEGENDS associated with Washington at Valley Forge, none is stranger than the so-called vision. On June 24, 1861, the *Philadelphia Inquirer* published an article titled "Washington's Vision," by one Wesley Bradshaw. On July 4, 1859, the author wrote, he had encountered a feeble, trembling ninety-nine-year-old veteran named Anthony Sherman in Independence Square in Philadelphia. After gazing wistfully upon Independence Hall, which he had come to see one final time before he died, Sherman asked Bradshaw to come with him inside and listen to a story. "I want to tell you an incident of Washington's life," he said, "one which no one alive knows of except myself, and if you live, you will, before long, see it verified."

The two men sat on an old wooden bench inside Independence Hall, and Sherman spoke about Valley Forge, the darkest period of the Revolutionary War. "I have even seen the tears coursing down our dear old commander's care-worn cheeks as he would be conversing with a confidential officer about the condition of his poor soldiers," he confided. Burdened with worries, Washington regularly used to whack his way into a thicket so that he could kneel and pray in private. One cold but sunny winter day, while Sherman stood guard outside, Washington spent the afternoon in his headquarters alone. He came out toward dusk looking pale and preoccupied, and stomped off to pray in the underbrush. He returned after dark and dispatched an orderly to summon an officer in whom he could confide. When the officer arrived, Washington sat down with him in his quarters and related a strange story that Sherman, perhaps crouching at the keyhole, over-heard.

"I do not know whether it was owing to the anxiety of my mind, or what," Washington told the officer, but that afternoon, as he sat at the table writing a letter, a feeling of unease had overtaken him. Looking up, he had seen a "sin-gularly beautiful female" standing in the room and gazing on him somberly. The general, who had given strict orders not to be disturbed and had not heard her enter, was at first too stunned to speak. When he finally found his tongue, he asked her what she wanted. She ignored him. Stammering, he asked her a second, third, and fourth time. She remained silent and slowly raised her eyebrows. Pinned by her power-ful gaze, Washington found that he could no longer speak or stand up, but could only gaze vacantly as she exerted her mas-tery over him. Soon he felt dizzy, and the room swam before his eyes. "Gradually, the surrounding atmosphere seemed as though becoming filled with sensations, and grew luminous. Everything about me appeared to rarify, the mysterious visi-tor herself becoming more airy, and yet more distinct to my sight than before." Washington thought he was dying, but remained powerless under the woman's irresistible spell.

"Son of the Republic," boomed a voice, "look and learn." The woman raised her arm and pointed to the east, where a heavy white mist rose and gradually dissipated to reveal all the lands of the earth. North America lay at the center; with the tossing, frothy waves of the Atlantic Ocean to the east and the Pacific Ocean to the west. "Son of the Repub-lic," again commanded the voice, "look and learn"; as the glassy-eyed general looked on, a "dark, shadowy, being like an angel," materialized over the Atlantic. Reaching down into the waves, it cupped water in each hand and sprinkled it on Europe and America. Instantly a cloud arose, hovered over the ocean, and then slowly drifted westward. Lightning struck from the cloud, and Washington heard the groans and shrieks of the American people. Fortunately, this rather serious thunderstorm did not last long before the angel sprinkled more water on the two continents and the cloud retreated, vanishing into the waves. As it departed, sunlight bathed the land, and towns and villages sprouted like dandelions from coast to coast.

Again the voice commanded the paralyzed son of the Republic to look and learn. From Africa, an "ill-omened" specter arose and drifted across the ocean to America, where it "flitted slowly" over the towns and villages. Crowds of miniature people—or so they must have appeared to Washington—responded by sallying forth and firing muskets or hacking at one another with swords. But the angels appeared to have a solution for every eventuality. Before long a bright angel appeared, wearing a luminous crown emblazoned "Union," and slammed a flag bearing the words "Remember, ye are brethren!" into the ground. In response the miniature people instantly tossed aside their weapons and united around the flag.

But the forces of evil were not through. The "dark, shadowy angel," evidently in league with the "ill-omened specter," pulled out a horn, blew three distinct blasts, and sprinkled water over Europe, Africa, and Asia. Terrified but still helpless, Washington looked on to see three black clouds arise from the besprinkled continents and merge together into one. Lit up by bolts of crackling, red lightning, the cloud trundled toward America. In the roiling black mist he could see "hordes of armed men, who, moving with the cloud, marched by land and sailed by sea to America." The cloud enveloped the continent, which echoed once more to "the thundering of cannon, clashing of swords and shouts and cries of the millions in mortal combat." Armies laid the land waste, and the little towns and cities burned like matchsticks. "Son of the Republic, look and learn," the voice cried yet again as the shadowy angel blew a "long, fearful blast" on his trumpet.

Looking up, Washington beheld a light as bright as a thousand suns piercing the dark cloud and shattering it into fragments. Down swept the bright angel, still fetchingly resplendent in its luminous crown, and bearing the flag in one hand and a sword in the other. Hundreds of "white spirits" followed, bent on combat, and joined the battle on behalf of the miniature Americans, who had verged on surrender. The battle ebbed and flowed until the voice bellowed for the last time, "Son of the Republic, look and learn." Again the shadowy angel splattered water across America; the clouds rolled back, and the invading armies disappeared. Towns and cities sprouted everywhere as the tiny people shouted and rejoiced and the bright angel planted his banner. Placing his crown atop the flagpole, he cried, "While the stars remain, and the heavens send down dew upon the earth, so long shall the Republic last." The people knelt and said amen.

As the scene faded, Washington looked up to see the mysterious woman still gazing sternly upon him. "Son of the Republic," she said, "what you have seen is thus interpreted: three perils will come upon the Republic. The most fearful is the second, passing which, the whole world united shall never be able to prevail against her. Let every child of the Republic learn to live for his God, his Land, and Union!" With these words she vanished, and Washington tumbled out of his seat, convinced, he told the officer, "that I had been shown the birth, progress, and destiny of the Republic of the United States. In Union she will have her strength, in Disunion her destruction."[32]

Wesley Bradshaw, the author of the article, was a pseudonym for Charles Wesley Alexander. At the beginning of the Civil War, Alexander published Washington's vision followed by *Jeff. Davis' Confession! A Singular Document Found on the Dead Body of a Rebel!* (1861). In February 1862 he published another episode of Washington's ghostly adventures, this time from the other side. Titled "General McClellan's Dream," it described how a "vapory mentor" appeared before the commander of the Army of the Potomac one night and warned him that treachery had caused a map of the defenses of Washington, D.C., to fall into Confederate hands. A few moments later, the form materialized into the "glorified and refulgent *Spirit of Washington*" and began describing the vision at Valley Forge while McClellan, "like a weak, dazzled bird . . . sat gazing at the heavenly vision." The spirit droned on for a while about union and liberty and then, after giving McClellan his "blessing" and "baptism of the spirit," disappeared. The Union general recovered to find a map covered with arrows and writings showing him how to confound the Confederates, and rode off to victory.[33]

These literary masterpieces complete, Alexander moved on to publish several tales of female Union soldiers with supernatural powers, and one of a demonic Englishwoman who fought for the South.[34] After the war, he wrote several classic penny dreadfuls with titles such as *Poor Ellen Stuart's Fate, or, Victim of the Free Love Institute in Oneida, N.Y.: A True and Thrilling Account of Miss Ellen Stuart's Captivity in a Free Love In-*

stitute, and Her Tragic Escape and Sufferings (1868) and *Ten Years of Torture: or Sutten's Death-bed Confession of How He Married Miss Martha Morton, an Accomplished Young Lady of Baltimore, with the Hellish Design of Torturing Her to Death, Merely Because She was Religious, While He Was an Infidel* (1871). Alexander found no place to insert Washington into these intriguing stories, but he made up for it by printing Washington's vision in several editions, including *The History and Legends of the Old Liberty Bell in Independence Hall in Philadelphia*, which came out for the Centennial in 1876.

The vision never happened, of course, and even Alexander probably did not at first expect anyone to take it as anything more than a childish story. The supposed narrator, Anthony Sherman, did not exist. The only known record for a soldier by that name serving in the Continental army refers to one Private Anthony Sherman or Shearman, who had been born in Massachusetts in 1752 and served in the New York line, received a pension in 1828, and died in 1830, before Alexander was born.[35] Even so, the story of Washington's vision persisted and grew in popularity over time. Northern newspapers reprinted it several times through the spring of 1862, and it appeared in pamphlet form, with a promotional blurb by the Massachusetts orator Edward Everett, in 1864. Nor did its popularity end with the conclusion of the Civil War. On March 14, 1871, the *Houston Daily Union* reprinted it verbatim, but with a title declaring that the three visions referred to the War of 1812, the Civil War, and another war impending in 1877. A Salt Lake City newspaper reprinted it again in 1877, but without reference to the war that the Houston newspaper had assumed would break out that year.[36]

The most significant republication, however, came in the December 1880 edition of the *National Tribune*, which had been established in 1877 as a newspaper for Union Civil War veterans. Although faithful for the most part to the 1861 edition, it introduced one important revision. In the 1861 article and the 1862 account of McClellan's dream, Alexander's ghostly woman had described the second trial as being by far the greatest America would have to face. In 1880, with the Civil War fifteen years in the past, she switched emphasis to the third vision. "Son of the Republic," she told Washington in the revised edition, "what you have seen is thus interpreted: Three great perils will come upon the Republic. The most fearful is the third, but in this greatest conflict the whole world united shall not prevail against her. Let every child of the Republic learn to live for his God, his land and the Union." Washington's final words changed, too, omitting the warning about disunion.[37]

The *National Tribune* version of the Valley Forge vision has proven the most popular. *Stars and Stripes* (once the *National Tribune*) reprinted it in 1931 and 1950. Mystical writer Manly P. Hall repeated the story of McClellan's dream, and Washington's ghostly role in it, in *The Secret Destiny of America* (1944). A Christian organization in Fairhope, Alabama, made the Valley Forge vision into an anti-Communist pamphlet in the 1950s, and the Pilgrim Tract Society of Randleman, North Carolina, distributed it from the 1960s through the 1980s. Susy Smith retold the legend in her book *Prominent American Ghosts* (1967), claiming wrongly that it had originally appeared in a Mormon periodical in 1856. And on February 21, 1961, ABC's science fiction television series *One Step Beyond* presented a bowdlerized version of the tale in which Washington, after encountering an Indian who tells him the legend of the Monongahela, passes into a trance and later describes his mystical vision to a doe-eyed Lafayette. Since then, the Valley Forge vision has become a staple of fringe groups, who herald the third vision as a prophecy of Armageddon comparable to the Bible's Book of Revelation.[38]

Catholic author Janice Connell offered a novel reinterpretation of the story in her book *Faith of Our Founding Father: The Spiritual Journey of George Washington* (2004). The mysterious woman who had hypnotized Washington at Valley Forge, Connell suggested, may have been the "Guardian Angel of the United States" or, more likely, none other than the Virgin Mary. After drawing the obvious parallel between the third vision and the so-called War on Terror, Connell also hinted that Washington "may have participated personally" in Catholic archbishop John Carroll's consecration of the United States to Mary in 1792, and that he may even have converted to Catholicism on his deathbed at the hands of a friendly local Jesuit priest. Though panned by critics, Connell's book sold better than some mainstream Washington biographies, and appeared in a new edition in 2007.[39]

IN THE 1920S AND 1930S, secularist debunkers attacked Christian-themed Washington legends with often intemperate fury. John Remsburg, an outspoken secularist and religious skeptic, set the tone early on in his book *Six Historic Americans* (1906). In it, he called Washington a "conscientious Deist" who made no more than a "few friendly allusions" to Christianity and never wrote "a single sentence that can with propriety be construed into an acknowledg-

ment of its claims." "Once or twice" only, claimed Remsburg, Washington referred to the faith in "complimentary
terms," and he never expressed any sentiment that "the safety
of the government or the happiness of the people depends
upon Christianity." To these statements Remsburg added
testimonials of Washington's refusal to take communion,
and suggested that reading between the lines of his correspondence showed Washington repeatedly asserting, "I am
not a Christian."[40]

Though provocative, Remsburg's writings did not receive wide distribution and were easily dismissed as the
work of a secularist hack. Subsequent attacks by debunkers
W. E. Woodward and Rupert Hughes were more difficult
to overlook. Woodward, who recast the adult Washington
in the image of a pragmatic Wall Street tycoon of the 1920s,
wrote, "He had no religious feeling himself, but thought
religion was a good thing for other people—especially for
the common people. Anyone who understands American
life will recognize the modern captain-of-industry attitude
in this point of view."[41] Hughes took on the prayer journal
and the "agonized wrestler in the snow" at Valley Forge,
exposing them both as fraudulent. Equating religiosity with
femininity, Hughes scoffed at the "schoolgirl virtues" that
tradition had ascribed to Washington. He suggested instead
that Washington's wife, "as often happens, furnished the religion for the family," and that the prayer journal had been
composed by another member of the family, "probably a
woman."[42] Hughes's friend Franklin Steiner took the same
tack in *The Religious Beliefs of Our Presidents* (1936), denouncing popular religious frauds while portraying Washington as
indifferent to religion or at most a deist.

For all their intensity, these secularist assaults failed to take root in the popular mind. The image of Washington at prayer reflected deep, resilient strains of piety and patriotism in American society. Woodward might rage all he liked at "the idea of this two-fisted man going about bellowing in the woods," but for many people, the image of the Founder on his knees in the snow, praying for deliverance at a moment of deep distress, was not silly but powerfully inspiring.[43] This remained true even during the iconoclastic 1960s and 1970s, when the image reappeared as a colossal statue at Valley Forge and on a national postage stamp.

RELIGIOUS WASHINGTON ICONOGRAPHY again became a subject for national debate when Barack Obama used the phrase "so help me God" as he took the presidential oath of office on January 20, 2009. The story that George Washington added the phrase to his own oath of office on April 30, 1789, has stood for generations. Historians David McCullough and Kenneth C. Davis have labeled the story authentic, and a video released by the Joint Congressional Committee on Inaugural Ceremonies, governed by the Senate Rules Committee, stated decisively that Washington used the phrase even though the Constitution did not mandate it. It is the standard today, and has been so at least since 1881, when Chester A. Arthur took his oath.[44]

A tradition dating from George Washington carries a lot more weight than one dating from the lowly Chester A. Arthur, and advocates of the phrase have strained every muscle to "prove" that Washington used it in 1789. The evidence is against them, however. There are no contemporary accounts indicating that Washington said "so help me God." Indeed, the Comte de Moustier, the French foreign minister, who stood near Washington as he took the oath and recorded it word for word, did not include the phrase in his meticulous account of the event. The first report that Washington used the phrase did not appear until 1854, in Rufus Wilmot Griswold's *The Republican Court, or, American Society in the Days of Washington.* Griswold, a poet and critic who made his name in part by slandering Edgar Allan Poe, was a serial plagiarist and literary scalawag. "Even while haranguing the loudest," complained a contemporary, Griswold was "purloining the fastest."[45]

Griswold's account of Washington's inauguration is a typical mid-nineteenth-century glob of treacle, supposedly adapted from the reminiscences of seventy-one-year-old Washington Irving, who had attended the event as a six-year-old boy. Washington "pronounced slowly and distinctly the words of the oath," said Griswold. "The Bible was raised, and as the President bowed to kiss its sacred pages, he said audibly, 'I swear,' and added, with fervor, his eyes closed, that his whole soul might be absorbed in the supplication, 'So help me God!'" To Irving, as Griswold quoted him, the act towered "solemn and awful beyond description . . . It seemed . . . to be a solemn appeal to Heaven and earth at once. In regard to this great and good man I may perhaps be an enthusiast, but I confess that I was under an awful and religious persuasion, that the gracious Ruler of the Universe was looking down at that moment with peculiar complacency on an act which to a part of his creatures was so very important."[46]

Griswold's account resembles all the other pieces of Washington hokum that sprouted up during the nineteenth century, from its heavy, breathless romanticism to its exaggeratedly precise detail. Irving repeated the tale in the fourth volume of his *Life of George Washington*, published in 1857, albeit without some of Griswold's embellishments.[47] He was a mere tyke at the time of the inauguration, however, and unlikely to have remembered the event with accuracy over six decades later. Moreover, not one of the hundreds of other people who allegedly witnessed Washington's supplication and reverent kissing of the Bible ever corroborated Irving's story. As with other tales, we must not only accept an old man's memories of early youth but also explain why the dramatic events he narrated were ignored by other eyewitnesses when they supposedly occurred.

We could explain this problem away—as many have done—by asserting a conspiracy of silence, but we might as well claim that Washington appeared at the inauguration dressed in women's clothing and that eyewitnesses were too embarrassed to mention it. Washington, a committed literalist in all matters of form, would have been extremely reluctant to append anything to the presidential oath of office—especially a religious addition, accompanied by dramatically pious gestures of the sort that he never made at any other point in his life. Some, seeking to cherry-pick the tale by discarding its more obviously ridiculous elements while preserving the core, have claimed that he may simply have said "so help me God" in a fit of absentmindedness, as it routinely formed an element of the many military oaths that he had taken throughout his life. But even this compromise strains credulity. First, and most obviously, why did a six-year-old boy, Irving, remember Washington using words and gestures that nobody else apparently noticed? And why did the Senate, on May 5, 1789, pass a bill that the House had approved on April 27, specifically excluding the words "so help me God" from congressional oaths of office? Would the senators have done so despite Washington's alleged public swoon over the Bible at his own inauguration six days earlier? Would Washington absentmindedly have added the words to his oath when the representatives had debated and then decided to strike out the words from their own oath just a few days earlier? Or would he have done so as a deliberate challenge to Congress over the place of religion in public life just as he entered office? And if so, why did Congress ignore him?[48]

In sum, any attempt to prove that Washington added the words "so help me God" requires mental gymnastics of the sort that would do credit to the finest artist of the flying trapeze. How much easier, then, just to assert over and over that it happened without making any attempt to justify it in the historical record and then appeal to it as a "tradition" that must never be broken. Such, at least, has been the approach taken by defenders of this story since its first appearance in 1854, and the results have met their desires. Since Chester Arthur in 1881, presidents have included the words in almost every known oath of office, with greater and lesser degrees of drama. Though atheists, secular humanists, and outraged academics occasionally pop up to protest, the tradition has become set in stone. To contravene it is not only to commit sacrilege but also, as Texas attorney general Greg Abbott told the *Washington Post* in 2009, to commence "the unraveling of society."[49]

CHAPTER 5

Washington Slept Here

Mɪssᴏᴜʀɪ ɴᴇᴡsᴘᴀᴘᴇʀᴍᴀɴ Rᴏʙᴇʀᴛᴜs Lᴏᴠᴇ set out in 1911 on a tour of the East Coast. He wanted to visit the sites of Washington's greatest military victories and gain insight into the source of his genius. But all he discovered was where Washington slept.

His first stop was Morristown, New Jersey, where Washington had shivered through two winter encampments. At the train station, Love asked the depot agent where he could find some sites and relics related to those periods. The agent's face lit up, and he swelled with civic pride. "Yes, indeed," he crowed. "There's the house where George Washington slept. Come right along and I'll show it to you."

Love next traveled to Freehold, New Jersey, near the site of the 1778 Battle of Monmouth. Locals steered him away from the battlefield and showed him where Washington slept.

At Trenton, Love crossed the Delaware on a bridge and discovered another of the commander in chief's bedchambers.
"I began to think," Love wrote, "that the entire state of New
Jersey must have been George Washington's bedroom. I wondered if George hung his nightshirt on Sandy Hook and did
all of his sleeping in New Jersey; if he always walked into that
state at bedtime—in his sleep—and went to bed." He soon
discovered otherwise.

Farther north, Love rode a train to New London, Connecticut. At the first house he entered, the proprietors dragged
him to a room where they said Washington had slept. They
hadn't made the bed since George tumbled out of it during the
Revolution. At Hartford, Love sought the famous charter oak,
but a local intercepted him to point out where Washington
had slept. The same happened in New Haven. In Waterbury,
renowned at that time as a center of the watchmaking industry, locals told him that Washington had used one of their
productions for an alarm clock because it ticked so loudly.
Over and over, in Rhode Island, Massachusetts, Vermont,
and finally New York City, Love learned more than he ever
wanted to know about the Founder's nocturnal habits. Washington, he concluded, "slept all the time. He slept twenty-four
hours a day. He never did anything but sleep. He never woke
up. And yet he whipped the British . . . just think what he
might have done had he been gifted with chronic insomnia!"[1]

BY 1911, the "Washington slept here" phenomenon had
become a standing national joke, but it had taken a long time
to reach that point. A hundred years earlier, Americans did
not worry overmuch about preserving historic buildings,

even those associated with the Founder, but they did trade in portable relics. In 1824, a Boston newspaper reported that the owner of a Newburyport home that Washington had visited in 1789 had preserved the "identical bed and bedding" on which the first president had slept. He sold it six years later.[2] Similarly, a Savannah, Georgia, newspaper reported in 1828 that a local family had preserved a down pillow that Washington had used during his visit to the city in 1790.[3] By midcentury, auction houses and curio dealers routinely sold both genuine and bogus Washington artifacts to an undiscriminating public. Homes and taverns where he had actually slept, meanwhile, fell into disrepair, including Mount Vernon.

The Revolutionary War centennial celebrations of the 1870s and 1880s helped to spur public interest in historic preservation, leading to what came to be dubbed the "historic homes movement." Many important buildings associated with the nation's founding, people realized, had fallen into ruins; some had already disappeared. Patriotic men and women decried the neglect and set about preserving or rebuilding. Their clumsy early efforts sometimes inflicted more damage than they repaired. In time, however, preservationists realized that proper reconstruction required some effort at achieving authenticity. The women of the Mount Vernon Ladies' Association, who took possession of Washington's estate in 1860 and protected it through the Civil War, set the standard in their meticulous restoration of buildings that had come perilously close to collapsing into total ruin.

Local reconstruction projects, though less professional, were often equally well intentioned. In 1897, a women's columnist for the *Philadelphia Inquirer* reported on how a group of young women had purportedly set about repairing a local house where Washington had slept. Before they arrived, it had been on the verge of falling to pieces. "It was a sin and a shame," the group's leader lectured her followers, "to let any house where George Washington had slept over night tumble down from sheer neglect when there were patriotic women in the neighborhood." With single-minded determination, the ladies raised funds by staging fairs and other entertainments— including a "1776 Congressional fancy ball"—and used the proceeds to hire workmen to fix up the place. Nothing deterred them, including an attempt to divert some of their funds into the construction of a new schoolhouse. Their work wasn't perfect, said one of the girls, but it stood "as a monument to the patriotic work that's being done in our society and to George Washington who slept there over night."[4]

Others were not quite so altruistic. Among the effects of the 1876 Centennial and succeeding commemorations was the growth of tourism, as Americans traveled up and down the East Coast to visit the homes of the Founders and the sites of their greatest exploits. Tourists meant money, and innkeepers and souvenir sellers eagerly competed for their business. Some were fortunate enough to own genuine Washington-associated homes, inns, and relics. Those who didn't could compensate simply by hanging up signs reading "Washington Slept Here" and assuming that tourists wouldn't know the difference either way. In most cases they were right. Tourists came, saw what they expected to see, and returned home with lighter wallets.

Even the owners of authentic properties found crafty means of increasing their trade, including installing bogus "period" furniture said to have been used by Washington, and making up anecdotes about things he had said or done during his visit. The owners of a summer resort at Schooley's Mountain in Morris County, New Jersey, attracted tourists by advertising the medicinal properties of their waters and claiming that Joseph Bonaparte—brother of the French emperor—and Ulysses S. Grant had visited there frequently. They also maintained a room in their Heath House Hotel where Washington allegedly had slept, and made a show of guarding its original fixtures.[5] The proprietors of the Blue Bell Inn near Philadelphia proudly told tourists how Washington had favored their establishment during the war or his presidency—accounts varied—and flirted with the serving girls. One night, they said, he had overheard the girls chattering about his good looks, and one of them exclaiming that she'd like to hold him in her arms and kiss him. Washington burst through the door and demanded to know which of them had said she wanted to kiss him. Stunned speechless, they stared at him goggle-eyed. "Then I will have to kiss all of you," he said, and promptly did so—although, the innkeepers hastened to add, "in that proper manner so becoming in the days of our grandfathers."[6]

MEMORIALIZING WASHINGTON's former haunts also boosted civic pride, bestowing bragging rights on city neighborhoods, towns, and rural communities. Visitors to Fredericksburg, Virginia, could not tour Washington's boyhood home along the Rappahannock, since it had burned down long ago, but they could learn all they wanted about the cherry tree. Washington had cut this down, of course, but dozens of new trees had sprouted from the original roots. "One often sees," a local historian noted in 1922, "a tourist cherishing a twig as a souvenir." Guides pointed out the sites of boyhood adventures related by Weems and other storytellers, including the point from which Washington had thrown a silver dollar across the Rappahannock (a story that likewise pleased early visitors to Mount Vernon on the Potomac).[7] Fredericksburg boasted the home of George's mother, Mary Washington, where she had lived for sixteen years before her death. Guides delighted their audiences by painting her as a villain and concocting outrageous tales of her perfidy. She was, they said, an outright Tory who denounced her son and declared for King George III. "George was always a good boy," they portrayed her as saying with a sarcastic sneer. "But I am afraid the King will yet catch him and hang him."[8]

Nor was the absence of a birthplace home insoluble. In 1815, George Washington Parke Custis dramatically placed a marble slab where he thought the old home had originally stood along Popes Creek. He then stood offshore in his private schooner and fired a cannon salute in the great man's honor. Annoyed farmers heaved the stone aside over the following years, and souvenir hunters hacked off fragments and carried them away. By 1870, it had disappeared entirely. In 1879, spurred by the Centennial celebrations, Congress appropriated money to survey Washington's birthplace. Two years later, Congress designated $30,000 for the construction of a new memorial, and in 1882 the Commonwealth of Virginia turned the property over to the federal government at no cost. Various holdups slowed the memorial project, but a fifty-foot granite obelisk was erected in 1896. Tourists finally had something to come and see.

Still, a slab of granite was just a slab of granite, and people could hardly be expected to go out of their way just to see it. In 1923, accordingly, Josephine Wheelwright Rust, a well-heeled Washington family descendant who lived a few miles from the birthplace, established the Wakefield National Memorial Association and charged it with the task of building a replica home near the site of the original building. The association quickly raised the necessary cash, and Rust's connections in Congress helped secure early passage of a bill granting permission to build a new home on the site. The stock market collapse of 1929 gutted the Wakefield Association's finances, temporarily putting a halt to building preparations, but the federal government swiftly stepped in. In January 1930, backed by a $65,000 congressional appropriation, President Herbert Hoover signed a bill establishing the George Washington Birthplace National Monument and turned over the task of constructing a replica home to the National Park Service. Rust and her association served in an advisory role.

There was only one problem. Although the Wakefield Association and the National Park Service had pledged themselves to build a "replica" of the original Washington home, no record existed of what the building had looked like. Horace Albright, the NPS director, pressed on regardless, and construction began immediately. Spurred by Rust and Albright's desire to finish in time for the bicentennial of Washington's birth, workers lovingly laid bricks fired out of local clay by brickmakers from Colonial Williamsburg, and plotted gardens according to a wholly imaginary conception of what their eighteenth-century equivalents had looked like. Josephine Rust died in June 1931, just a few months before the project was complete, but her passing added poignancy to a special memorial service for Washington at the homestead on February 11, 1932.

At least she was spared the embarrassments to follow. Archaeologists, who had already expressed private doubts about the project's veracity, solemnly pronounced in 1936 that the "replica" Rust had expended so much effort to construct was wildly inaccurate. It was, they said, made out of the wrong materials, much too large, and sited in the wrong place. And it need never have been built. During its construction, workers had uncovered the nearby foundations of some eighteenth-century buildings. They seemed much too small for the Washington family, and overseers hurriedly ordered the excavations to be filled in. Nagging doubts nevertheless worried the memorial's superintendents, and in 1936 they conscripted a local crew from the Civilian Conservation Corps to perform a careful excavation and completely uncover the foundations. Their conclusions were irrefutable: undeniably, Washington's original home had once stood here. Embarrassed recriminations flew, but too late. The NPS revised its sign at the new building to read "this house is neither a reproduction nor a facsimile of the original," but it remained the birthplace memorial's centerpiece. Controversy raged among academics and other purists, but their complaints remained behind the scenes, and over the following decades millions of tourists tiptoed respectfully through the new building, unaware that it bore no relation to Washington's actual childhood home. Locals couldn't complain—the throngs of visitors contributed mightily to their community's income.[9] Today, visitors to Washington's birthplace may visit both the reconstructed buildings—accurately labeled as "not true replicas"—and the

original foundations, along with a more authentic re-creation
of a colonial-era plantation.

FOR ALL THE POMP and display surrounding the Washington
memorials at Fredericksburg, Alexandria undoubtedly held
the best claim to Washington's legacy. By the last decades
of the nineteenth century, Alexandria swarmed with guides.
They led visitors to Market Square, where Washington drilled
troops; Gadsby's Tavern, where he drank and danced; and
Christ Church, where he worshiped. They also traipsed to
places where Washington had never been—but who could
tell the difference? The better the stories they told, the bigger
their tips. A typical example of their zany stories goes: "General Washington was coming from church one day, and he
saw a pretty little white thing in the road, and shot at it. The
thing shot back in its peculiar way, and General Washington
had to bury his clothes. A man makes nothing by fighting
with skunks."[10] At the same time Alexandrians gave their city
a thorough makeover, transforming what had been a dingy,
decaying southern backwater into a clean and relatively safe
tourist destination that boasted well-preserved historic buildings along with the latest modern conveniences.

No visit to Alexandria was complete without a tour of
nearby Mount Vernon, but there would have been little to
visit had it not been for the efforts of Ann Pamela Cunningham and the organization she founded, the Mount Vernon
Ladies' Association of the Union. The quiet but steel-willed
daughter of a wealthy South Carolina planter, Cunningham
was thirty-seven years old when she rode a river steamer
down the Potomac past Mount Vernon late in 1853. Look-

ing shoreward, she saw Washington's once-proud estate in an advanced state of dilapidation and decay. "Why," she asked herself, "was it that the women of his country did not try to keep it in repair, if the men could not do it?" Others had posed similar questions, but Cunningham followed through.

Founding the Ladies' Association, Cunningham launched a grassroots campaign across the South, asking women to donate funds for the purchase and restoration of Mount Vernon. As money poured in, Cunningham decided to expand the campaign from a regional cause to a national one, and invited Yankee women to participate as well. Supported by celebrities such as Washington Irving and the famous orator Edward Everett, the campaign succeeded beyond anyone's expectations. Just four years after its foundation—and two years ahead of schedule—the association possessed more than adequate funds to complete the purchase. John Augustine Washington III, the estate's owner, initially refused to sell, but after Cunningham converted his wife to the cause, he caved in. He signed Mount Vernon—with an estate of 200 acres, down from the 8,000 acres that Washington had acquired by the end of his life—over to the association on April 6, 1858.

The Civil War prevented any large-scale restoration at Mount Vernon, as the Ladies' Association focused on protecting it from destruction by either of the opposing armies. Even after the war's end, the ladies had to devote a considerable part of their time and resources to protecting Washington's estate from the hands of his countrymen. "Americans are more destructive as visitors than any other nationality," Cunningham wrote fretfully, "so more men are needed here to watch our visitors. . . . Do what we will, however, with the force we have kept, we cannot prevent clippings outside and pilfering inside, in the rooms shown to visitors. The cornices are constantly broken off, even the ivory on the keys of the celebrated harpsichord are taken off, though a man stands in that room to protect the things exhibited there."[11] This problem grew larger and more complex as the Centennial approached and hordes of tourists began visiting the estate. Fences had to be built around the larger trees to prevent people from tearing off bark, and rooms closed from time to time in order to repair plundered fittings. But these restrictions angered visitors. They believed that paying for tickets entailed the right to tour every part of the estate. Irate guests forced increased security, which in turn fostered further resentment.

The problem, in part, was that Cunningham and her fellow ladies thought ahead of their time. Their intentions were simple and straightforward: preserve, restore, and honor Washington's estate as a national shrine. True, their interior decorations did not always conform to eighteenth-century norms, and their understanding of Washington the man reflected many of the prejudices and misconceptions of their times. But they were not in it for profit and never willfully deceived in order to attract more visitors. For most nineteenth-century Americans, however, tourism and souvenir hunting went hand in hand. They stripped Civil War monuments of their ornaments or hacked them to pieces just a few years after they had been erected, and they looted historic buildings mercilessly, sometimes to the brink of disintegration. Americans' burning need to personalize Washington magnified this problem for the Ladies' Association and other keepers of his legacy. People craved some connection with the Founder, and relics served to introduce him as an immediate presence into their lives. Looted relics could be either kept and prized or sold profitably to other collectors. The same urge drove charlatans to forge letters, sell phony relics, tell tall tales, and hang up "Washington Slept Here" signs.

Ann Pamela Cunningham died in 1875, after tearfully exhorting her successors to "let no irreverent hand change [Mount Vernon]; no vandal hands desecrate it with the fingers of 'progress'! Those who wish to go to the home where he lived and died, wish to see in what he lived and died! Let one spot in this grand country of ours be saved from change!"[12] As Mount Vernon grew in prominence, becoming the nation's number one tourist magnet, the Ladies' Association remained firmly devoted to authenticity. But they were human and presented Washington according to their lights. Susan Fenimore Cooper, daughter of the novelist, declared in 1858 as she solicited funds for the Ladies' Association that Mount Vernon must be held up as the model of a "Christian home, with all its happy blessings, its sacred restraints," and Washington's tomb should be a "Christian grave."[13] The ladies endorsed this view and presented visitors with a highly idealized vision of Washington's family life as a manifestation of the purest Christian virtue. Furnishings—most of them replicas or antiques acquired elsewhere—were arranged with an eye to inducing a sense of cozy domesticity, and with the instinctive Victorian affinity for clutter.[14]

Slavery presented the Ladies' Association with a particularly sensitive issue. Shortly after the purchase of the estate in 1858, an advisor to the association had recommended the demolition of all the surviving buildings at Mount Vernon except for the mansion and the tomb. The outbuildings, he suggested, were the homes and workplaces of "menials"—that is, slaves—and had no real historical value. Fortunately, Cunningham and the Ladies' Association turned down this advice and did what they could to preserve the decaying outbuildings. As at other historic sites in the country, however, slavery had no role in the story presented to Mount Vernon's visitors. This remained the case until the mid-twentieth century: the Ladies' Association erected a memorial stone at an old slave graveyard in 1929 and began reconstructing the original slave quarters in 1950–51.[15]

In Alexandria and the surrounding region, Mount Vernon–related tourism proved a tremendous boon for guides, merchants, and innkeepers, who employed all means fair and foul to keep 'em coming. But in nearby Washington, D.C., the influx of tourists and foreign dignitaries to celebrate the Centennial caused some embarrassment. With the nation in a craze for all things Washington, and domestic and foreign tourists crawling all over the place looking for sights and souvenirs, the Washington Monument, begun in 1833, remained incomplete. Stuck since 1859 at 156 feet, or less than a third of its projected height, it was a national laughingstock. Ironically, even as Ann Pamela Cunningham raked in piles of cash to preserve and restore Mount Vernon, hardly a penny could be found to finish the Washington Monument. The reasons for this included the superior ability and determination of Cunningham's ladies and the wishy-washy incompetence of the men backing the Washington Monument. But there can be no doubt that Americans found Mount Vernon a more attractive cause for the simple reason that it humanized Washington by returning him to his home. Why erect a huge but impersonal marble obelisk to a man who had already been encased in a kind of national sepulcher? As an editorial writer for the *New York Tribune* opined in 1875, "Public judgment on that abortion [the Washington Monument] has been made up. The country has failed in many ways to honor the memory of its first President, but the neglect to finish this Monument is not to be reckoned among them. A wretched design, a wretched location, and an insecure foundation match well with an empty treasury." Politicians called openly for it to be blown up and carted away.[16]

No grassroots movement emerged to save the Washington Monument. But in 1874–76, Dr. Otis H. Tiffany embarked on a national lecture tour to trumpet the glories of Washington, with the aim of convincing Congress to get the thing finished. A Methodist minister at the Metropolitan Church in Washington, D.C., Tiffany sported bizarre tufted sideburns but was a fiery orator, and counted President Grant among his flock. Grant attended Tiffany's lecture on Washington in Baltimore, and in August he signed a $200,000 funding bill for the monument that had just passed through Congress. The bill stipulated that the monument should be finished by 1881, the anniversary of Yorktown, but the capstone was not laid until December 1884. President Chester A. Arthur led the dedication ceremonies on February 21, 1885, invoking "the immortal name and memory of George Washington." Crowds of spectators crunched through a light covering of snow, huddling against the cold as they gazed up at the 555-foot-tall monolith, and then followed a military procession to the Capitol, where orators beguiled a miscellaneous assemblage of politicians and Washington descendants.[17]

It was all old-school George Washington: proud, austere, distant, just like the monument itself. Newspapers gave great play to the monument's construction and dedication, boasted of its status—only briefly maintained—as the highest structure in the world, touted its electric lighting (provided by the Edison Company), and extolled the engineering know-how displayed in its construction. Daredevils talked of diving off the monument, and an "expert baseball player" tried and failed to catch a baseball dropped from the top. "The ball came down with such velocity," reported an observer, "that his hands were forced apart, and the ground below was dented as if struck by a cannon ball."[18] But the monument inspired no renewal of interest in Washington's life, personality, and achievements.

OUTSIDE THE DISTRICT OF COLUMBIA and northern Virginia, Americans found less daunting means of linking up with Washington, boosting civic pride, and attracting tourists. Their activities—which could be as simple as installing a tablet next to an old tree stump or digging up refuse and announcing that Washington had thrown it away—imbued the Founder with a sense of cozy familiarity that the monument in Washington, D.C., could never inspire. Residents of Yorktown, Virginia, made up for the absence of the commander in chief's original headquarters building, which had burned down, by directing visitors to the stump of an old mulberry tree that Washington had allegedly slept under every night during the siege, using its roots for his pillow.[19] The story proved especially useful in attracting tourists to the town during the centennial of the siege, in 1881. In Wallingford, Connecticut, residents claimed that Washington had slept on the night of October 18, 1789, at the town's Washington Hotel—actually he had only breakfasted there—and dug up a rather dubious relic to back up their claim. One day in February 1885 Dwight Hall, an elderly retired colonel from Wallingford, poked around in the dirt behind the hotel and came up with a rusty old key. Washington, he instantly proclaimed, had used it to lock his door on the night he allegedly slept there. Town authorities declared the key a "precious relic," and the old colonel announced that he would have it framed, plated in silver, and sent to President Grover Cleveland as a gift.[20]

Skilled orators emphasized the profoundly personal relationship of antique houses and relics with the original Washington. In 1873, a house that Washington had tenanted in Morristown, New Jersey, went up for sale. Huge crowds gathered to bid on the building and its contents, including household furniture that he had allegedly used and a Masonic sash that he had supposedly left behind in a fit of forgetfulness. Sensing the value of these objects and the building as a beacon for civic pride—and tourists—a group of wealthy citizens pooled their resources and purchased the entire lot. They then formed a hereditary organization under state charter, the Washington Association of New Jersey, to maintain the house in perpetuity. Speaking to a rally at the house in 1875, former governor Theodore Randolph irresistibly evoked George and Martha Washington's personal connection with the place:

> The same oaken doors open to you as they did to Washington; the massive knocker his hand was wont to touch yet waits obedient to your wish. The floors he trod in anxious thought with wearied brain, you may tread. . . . The dwelling was for many months the home of Martha. . . . Within these rooms, with quiet dignity and grace,

she received her husband's guests. . . . The curious old secretary he used, with its hidden drawers and quaint workmanship, stands here now as it did then. The mirrors used by General and Lady Washington you may see your faces reflected in. The old camp chest, heavy and solid, is yet good for a long campaign.[21]

Proprietors of this and other houses took particular pleasure in displaying Washington's bed, often with the "original" tumbled bedclothes. "Near the site of the battle of Trenton," reported a journalist, "there are dozens of antique enthusiasts who claim ownership of the bed in which Washington slept the night before he crossed the Delaware."[22] Thousands of Washington's chamber pots were also coyly displayed.

Anecdotes connected Washington not just to objects and homes but to towns and even regions. Many, if not most, were mythical, but since they humanized Washington and revealed local citizens in a flattering light, they proved enduringly popular. Baltimoreans told of how two boys had observed Washington at a public event during his presidency and then boldly snuck past guards to waylay him in his own bedchamber. Barging into his room, they proudly displayed hats bearing white cockades, which indicated support for Jefferson's Republicans. Far from taking offense, Washington mildly offered to craft replacement cockades for the lads. He then ordered a servant to procure a piece of black ribbon, cut Federalist cockades, and placed them in the boys' hats. They left the room avowed Federalists.[23]

In Trenton, New Jersey, locals spoke of how Washington sat on an empty, wooden beehive, wrapped in his cloak, watching his troops cross the Delaware during the night of

December 25, 1776, and then enjoined them to "fight like men." As the fighting began, they said, he raised his sword and shouted out orders, and at that moment a musket ball passed between his fingers. "*That* has passed by," he sardonically remarked. On another occasion at Morristown, people said, an inebriated young bon vivant burst into Washington's headquarters shrieking that the British were attacking, throwing the entire staff into a panic until the commander in chief silenced them all with a booming "Be quiet!"[24] In Philadelphia, an elderly resident told visitors an anecdote of Washington at the local fish market:

> Once . . . Washington walked among the fish stands at the foot of Market Street. "Auntie, that is a fine shad you have there," pointing to a fat one in the fishwoman's basket. "Yes, General, and let me send it home for you." "No," said he, "put a string through its gill. I reckon a man can carry his own grub home." The good woman therefore tied a string through the gills, and off the General started with his fish in one hand and his cane in the other. And as he passed along towards his home at Sixth and Market Streets, he found for once that he had undertaken almost more than even he could well accomplish; for at every step a hat would be raised in his honor, and of course the General's was to be removed in response. This he found no easy task, but he soon solved the difficulty by placing his hat under his arm, and was thus enabled to bow bareheaded to those who saluted him.[25]

Skenesborough, New York, proudly boasted the biggest and most venomous mosquitoes in North America, and called on Washington as a witness. Passing through one day, locals said, a mosquito-harried Washington despairingly cried that they could "bite through the thickest boot."[26]

Minor anecdotes such as these could be repeated endlessly. Each locality had its own. Most have disappeared in the wisps of time, but the more dramatic examples would fascinate and mislead visitors for decades to come. All placed Washington's greatest exploit, or lucky escape, just at that spot—and usually thanks to the efforts of some humble local citizen. Among the most influential of these, sanctified to the present day by no less an authority than *Encyclopedia Britannica* and scores of local and popular history books, is the story of the Quaker widow who saved Washington's army.

On December 2, 1777, Washington's army was at White-marsh, Pennsylvania, recuperating from a brutal campaigning season. The weather grew colder and the season's first snows fell as the commander in chief prepared to shift his troops to Valley Forge. But the fighting had not ended yet. In Philadelphia, which His Majesty's forces had occupied on September 26, British general William Howe prepared a surprise attack on the Americans. He had established his headquarters on Second Street in the city, and his officers commandeered quarters in several of the surrounding homes. One of these was 177 South Second Street, the home of Irish Quakers William and Lydia Darragh, who had arrived in America in 1775. Lydia, who in 1777 was about forty-nine years old, contributed to the family income by working as a midwife and sewing grave clothes. She, like her husband, was a pacifist and officially neutral in the conflict but, so the story went, secretly sympathized with the patriots.

On the evening of December 2, the British officers in

the house—including Adjutant General John André, whom Washington later would have executed after the defection of Benedict Arnold—ordered the Darragh family to retire to their rooms. Ostentatiously—and rather foolishly—the officers declared that they had "secret" business to attend to in another part of the house, and did not want to be disturbed. Undeterred, Mrs. Darragh waited for the officers to retire and then took off her shoes and tiptoed down the hall. Listening at the keyhole, she overheard the officers discussing a plan for a sneak attack on Washington's army. When they finished, she silently went back to her room and pretended to be asleep when one of the officers came knocking a few minutes later.

That night and all the following day, the story went, Mrs. Darragh paced nervously about, unable to eat or sleep. As a Quaker, she did not feel able to take sides, yet the lives of thousands of Americans depended on her. And her son was an officer in Washington's army! She made up her mind—she would reveal her secret to the Americans. Refusing to confide in her husband, she feigned a desperate need for flour, which for some reason could only be procured behind American lines. General Howe agreeably provided Mrs. Darragh with a pass, and quick as a wink she darted past the pickets and accosted the first American she met. This, according to the storytellers, was one Lieutenant Colonel Craig of the Light Horse. Begging Craig not to betray her name, even to his superiors, Mrs. Darragh revealed the British plan. Craig was amazed by the incredible news, and after thanking her he vaulted onto his pony and charged off to tell Washington. The commander in chief, all unsuspecting up to this point, uncritically accepted the woman's information and redeployed his army to repel the British attack. Howe arrived on December 5, found Washington strongly entrenched, and discreetly withdrew. Lydia Darragh, the humble Quaker Irishwoman from Philadelphia, had saved Washington's army and the Revolution.

André, baffled at the failure of Howe's masterly plan, wondered if he had been betrayed. Had one of the Darraghs disregarded his strict order not to eavesdrop on their top-secret conversation and listened outside the door, where he had inexplicably neglected to place a sentry? Mrs. Darragh had since returned from her flour-gathering mission across the lines, and he asked her up to his room. She obeyed, and trembled fearfully as André locked the door and with an air of mystery asked her to be seated. Had any of the family been up the night of December 2, he asked, during their secret meeting? No, she cried, they had all gone to bed at eight o'clock as ordered. André rubbed his chin, perplexed. Surely this woman could not lie. "I know *you* were asleep," he mused, "for I knocked at your door three times before you heard me. I am entirely at a loss to imagine who gave General Washington information of our intended attack, unless the walls of the house could speak!" Mrs. Darragh, savior of America, escaped detection, and went on to live a happy and prosperous life before passing away in 1789.[27]

The origins of this romance are as hazy as those of any other Washington legend. In 1827, one Robert Walsh published the story for the first time in the *American Quarterly Review*, attributing it to "several most respectable persons of our acquaintance, and implicitly believed by all of them, who knew her character and situation."[28] Later writers claimed to have heard it from friends of Lydia Darragh or from her great-granddaughter, who attested in the early 1900s that Lydia had hidden intelligence reports behind her fourteen-year-old son John's coat buttons. John then carried the reports across the lines to his older brother Charles, who presented them personally to Washington. Lydia herself never left a scrap of writing in support of the claim, which seemed to rest upon nothing more than family tradition—the same anonymous "experts" and distant relations who certified most other legends of this sort.

There was, however, some partially corroborating evidence. In 1894, a Philadelphia publishing house printed *Journal or Historical Recollections of American Events During the Revolutionary War*, which had been taken from a copy of a manuscript written long after the war by Elias Boudinot. At the time of the Whitemarsh affair, Boudinot had been Washington's commissary general of prisoners. On December 2, contemporary documents show that Boudinot was in Philadelphia inspecting the condition of American prisoners in that city, and he almost certainly did not return to Whitemarsh in time to witness the skirmishing there. But Boudinot, whose rambling and self-serving account of the war always placed him in the heat of the action, with critical responsibilities, gave a very different version of the period.

On December 3, Boudinot wrote, he not only served Washington as commissary general of prisoners but "managed the Intelligence of the Army." (This was untrue: in 1779 he took a small role in intelligence gathering, but not in 1777, and at no time did he—or anyone else, for that matter—"manage" Washington's intelligence service.) Riding around Philadelphia, gathering information, Boudinot happened upon a "poor looking insignificant old woman"—Lydia Darragh, remember, was about forty-eight—who wanted to go into the country to buy flour. After he finished questioning her, she thrust "a dirty old needle-book, with various small pockets in it," into his hands and hobbled away. In the back of the needle book Boudinot discovered a piece of paper rolled up tightly into a "pipe shank," which he unrolled. It reported that Howe was on his way to Whitemarsh with 5,000 men. Boudinot informed Washington and saved the army.[29]

There are dozens of details in these two accounts that do not ring true, including the unaccountable stupidity of André—an experienced and savvy officer—in letting his conference be overheard; the nonexistence of a "Lieutenant Colonel Craig of the Light Horse"; Boudinot's false statement about "managing" Washington's intelligence service and his probable presence in Philadelphia supervising arrangements for the prisoners; and above all the well-documented fact that Washington had already heard of the impending attack from several other sources before December 3. Women did on many occasions provide intelligence during the Revolutionary War, and Lydia Darragh might have supplied information to Washington on this or other occasions. But qualified suppositions are never enough when people crave a really good story.

Although the particulars of the Darragh affair as related by Boudinot and the *American Quarterly Review* were almost certainly fantasy, they appealed to the vanity of Philadelphians. They also made excellent fodder for overworked schoolteachers seeking—then as now—to "make history fun." "The Darragh romance . . . appealed particularly to the fancy of Philadelphia," wrote author Thompson Westcott in 1877, because "the house on Second Street, below Spruce, in which the heroine lived, was still standing. It came to be

pointed out with much veneration, while she herself provided a theme to which school teachers never found their
pupils weary of listening."[30] Westcott's efforts to debunk
the legend—which he claimed had most likely originated
in the frenzy of local storytelling that coincided with Lafayette's visit to the city in 1824—proved fruitless. In 1916
the City History Society of Philadelphia published a booklet
by Henry Darrach (no relation to the Darraghs) declaring
definitively that the legend rested on "trustworthy sources"
and arguing curiously that "the truthfulness of the story does
not depend upon successfully answering objections made to
it." Eventually the tale became a matter not just of Phila-
delphian but of female pride, receiving uncritical treatment
in Melissa Bohrer's *Glory, Passion, and Principle: The Story of
Eight Remarkable Women at the Core of the American Revolution*
(2003) and Elizabeth Leonard's *All the Daring of the Soldier:
Women of the Civil War Armies* (1999). It also appears on the
website of the National Women's History Museum and in a
History Channel documentary shown in the Mount Vernon
educational center.

ANOTHER BELOVED PHILADELPHIA TRADITION is the story of
Betsy Ross. In 1870, old Betsy's grandson William Canby
addressed the Pennsylvania Historical Society. "To Philadelphia," he boldly proclaimed, "belongs the honor of having
first flung the 'Star Spangled Banner' to the breeze, and . . . to
a Philadelphia lady, long since gathered to her fathers, belongs
the honor of having made the first flag with her own hands."
One day in the spring of 1776, he said, Betsy had been sitting in her upholstery shop, quietly sewing with her young

daughters, when four men walked in. She immediately recognized the "handsome form and features of the dignified,
yet graceful and polite Commander in Chief," for he was
an old friend who had often come by on social and business
visits during the French and Indian War. The other three
introduced themselves as members of a secret committee of
Congress who had it in charge to design a new flag for the
United States. Could she make one? they asked. In humble
reply, she said that she did not know but she would try.

Moving to the back room, Mrs. Ross and the four men
hashed out a design. Washington made all the suggestions
except one. But when the men called for six-pointed stars,
assuming that they would be simpler to sew, Mrs. Ross de-
murred. The stars should have five points, she said, and when
the men hesitated, suggesting that the work might prove too
difficult, she muttered, "Nothing easier," and swiftly clipped
a five-pointed star out of a piece of paper. As they left, Washington and the congressmen asked her to make a sample flag
and present it to them in a few days. This she did, using a
painting by a local artist and an old ship's standard as guides.
At the appointed time, she strolled down to the city wharf
and had a shipmaster run her creation up his flagpole. The
committee members—Washington, evidently, was not in
attendance—and bystanders gasped in admiration, and by
general consent the flag was approved as the new banner of
the United States. On the following day the committee appointed Mrs. Ross the national seamstress and provided her
with funds to produce all the nation's flags. "This is too good
luck for me," she sighed, "it cannot be." But, she continued,
"we are not creatures of luck: have I not found that the Good
One has never deserted me, and He will not now." She set to

work and churned out star-spangled banners for the remainder of the war.

In relating this story, to which he and other members of the Ross family would swear affidavits of authenticity, Canby called his audience's attention to "a little two story and attic house, with over-hanging eaves and pent-eaves, and a porch at the door, the brick front decorated with alternate glazed bricks, situated on the North side of Arch Street a few doors East of Third street." This "unpretending and humble abode," he informed them, had once had a little tin sign in its window reading "Elizabeth Ross Upholsterer." It marked "the birth place of the Star-spangled Banner." Through the windows, he said, passersby might still see original specimens of Mrs. Ross's work—no flags, but pillows, embroidery, and other needlework. Visitors might also imagine watching the quaint and peaceful features of old Betsy and her daughters as they went about their patriotic work.[31]

Locals took the hint. Shortly after Canby's presentation, the Betsy Ross house became a place of pilgrimage and a prime tourist attraction. German immigrants by the name of Mund owned the house, and they turned it into a tavern, hanging up a sign reading "First Flag of the US Made in this House." They did especially good business during the 1876 Centennial, putting out advertisements such as "Original Flag House, Lager, Wine and Liquors. This is the house where the first United States flag was made by Mrs. John Ross." As the colonial-era houses nearby crumbled, locals began to fear that the Ross house would succumb to the elements as well. In 1898, therefore, a group of citizens led by Charles Weisgerber organized the American Flag House and Betsy Ross Memorial Association, raised funds locally, and purchased the house from the Munds. Weisgerber moved his family into the home, opened two rooms to the public, and ran a souvenir concession. Another local drive funded a massive restoration project in 1937, and four years later the house was donated to the City of Philadelphia. It remains a popular attraction. In 2009, television's *Ghost Hunters* show did its part to induce tourism by "discovering" in the course of a Syfy channel broadcast that a ghost, presumably that of old Betsy herself, roamed the halls of her old abode and spooked unwary guests.

The current managers of the house leave it up to their visitors to decide whether the flag story is "historical fact or well-loved legend." They are prudent to do so, for Canby's tale is entirely imaginary. Betsy Ross did at one time make flags—but in 1777, and for the Pennsylvania State Navy Board. Washington did visit Philadelphia briefly in early June 1776, but he did not meet during that time with Congress or anyone else in order to discuss flags. He most likely did not know Betsy Ross, and certainly didn't make social calls on her in the 1750s. There was no secret committee. And Canby's vociferous claim that the national flag had flapped in the breeze at Philadelphia's wharf *before* the Declaration of Independence is false. To the contrary, Congress did not adopt a national flag until June 14, 1777. Francis Hopkinson, an artist and poet who signed the Declaration of Independence, probably designed it.[32]

PHILADELPHIA LAID CLAIM to many, but by no means all, of the best Washington fables. In New Jersey, the story of Revolutionary War spy John Honeyman fostered state pride and enlivened history books. It went as follows. In 1775

Honeyman, a tall, muscular Irishman, offered his services to Washington, who immediately took him into his complete confidence. Honeyman, he knew, had served as General James Wolfe's right-hand man in 1759 at the famous assault on Quebec, and had earned a reputation as one of the country's most remarkable soldiers. An opportunity to make use of Honeyman's services arose one year later, in the autumn of 1776, when British forces exploded out of northern Manhattan and swarmed across New Jersey. Washington needed a good spy to keep tabs on their activities. Who better than Honeyman? From his service under Wolfe he had become intimately acquainted with the British Army, and because his family had settled in Somerset County he was familiar with the land. Washington ordered him to pose as a butcher with Tory sympathies, and sent him off.

Mid-December 1776 found Honeyman at Trenton, then occupied by Hessians under the command of Colonel Johann Rall. For several days Honeyman prowled around the town, a cart whip in one hand, a rope in the other, and a greasy old coat on his back, ostensibly looking for stray cows but actually taking careful notes of enemy dispositions. After culling all the information he could, Honeyman arranged to be captured by some American pickets along the Delaware River. He acted his part well, screaming that he was only a poor butcher trying to support his family as the Americans tied him up and dragged him to headquarters. Washington, who had told his soldiers to look out for such a man, received Honeyman gravely. He was, the general told his assembled officers, a dangerous spy, and must be interrogated closely.

Washington sent his men out, telling them to shoot the butcher if he tried to escape, and spoke with Honeyman alone for about ninety minutes. In private, the disguise dropped, and Honeyman breathlessly told the general of Rall's dispositions and utter unpreparedness for a fight. When their conference ended, Washington ordered Honeyman into close confinement. He then quietly made arrangements for his escape. That night, a fire broke out some distance away from the guardroom, and all the guards ran over to attend it. When they returned, the door to Honeyman's cell remained locked, but in the morning the guards discovered that he was not inside. Washington raged and fumed, but it was too late.

Three days later, Washington crossed the Delaware and won his famous victory at Trenton. Honeyman, his cover secure, continued to pose as a Tory and gather intelligence. His family's patriot neighbors considered him a perfidious swine, and on several occasions they attempted to lynch his family. Each time his wife fended them off by brandishing a letter from Washington himself, which read: "To the good people of New Jersey: It is hereby ordered that the wife and children of John Honeyman, of Griggstown, the notorious Tory, now within the British lines, and probably acting the part of a spy, shall be and hereby are protected from all harm and annoyance from every quarter, until further orders. But this furnishes no protection to Honeyman himself." The note cleverly ensured the safety of Honeyman's family while maintaining his cover as a Tory spy. His services continued until the end of the war, when Washington visited and thanked him personally in the presence of a large crowd.

Thus the story. It appeared for the first time in 1873, in the form of an article by John Van Dyke in *Our Home* magazine. Van Dyke, a former state congressman and New Jersey Supreme Court justice, was Honeyman's grandson. He claimed to have known his grandfather well, and to have attended at his death in 1822. Van Dyke did not, however, profess to have heard the details of this tale from the old soldier personally. Instead, he had consulted the usual unnamed but "most unmistakable sources." In essence, then, the Honeyman story amounted to just another family legend. No documentation— including the letter that Washington had supposedly written to Honeyman's wife, which Van Dyke quoted verbatim—ever turned up, and no witnesses to Washington's supposed visit to the spy ever appeared. Family historian A. Van Doren Honeyman even admitted that John Honeyman himself had never said a word about his wartime services.

But these were minor details. The Honeyman tale was a matter of local pride and was lovingly recounted in the family history published in 1909. In his retelling, Van Dyke boasted to his readers that upon New Jersey's "own soil, and among its own people . . . there lived and died a spirit . . . faithful and brave," who embarked on "romantic, perilous and important" adventures in Washington's personal service. William S. Stryker, the state historian, repeated the story in his book *The Battles of Trenton and Princeton* (1898), and popular historian Leonard Falkner retold it with numerous embellishments in an *American Heritage* article in 1957. From there it found its way into Richard Ketchum's *The Winter Soldiers* (1973) and numerous other history books. It even deceived debunker Rupert Hughes.[33] The CIA has enshrined the story on the section of its website chronicling the history of American espionage.

*   *   *

REGIONAL PRIDE—as opposed to civic or state pride—also inspired a slew of legends. In 1838, Virginia governor James McDowell, a renowned orator, spoke at a commencement ceremony at the College of New Jersey (later Princeton University). Frothing and gesticulating with an eloquence modeled after that of state hero Patrick Henry, McDowell recalled the assembled students to those dark days of 1776, just before the Battles of Trenton and Princeton. With his army in disarray and the enemy pressing in on all sides, Washington knew the end might be at hand. But he also had a place of refuge in mind: the misty mountains of western Virginia, where he had roved as a young surveyor. "Strip me of the wretched and suffering remnant of my soldiers," the general declared; "take from me all I have left; leave me a standard; give me but the means of planting it upon the mountains of West Augusta, and I will yet draw around me the men who will lift up their bleeding country from the dust and set her free."[34]

Back home in Virginia, people heard of McDowell's invention—for invention it was—and repeated it in endless variations. Caperton Braxton, another feisty orator, repeated the quote at a joint meeting of the American and Virginia Bar Associations at Hot Springs, Virginia, in 1903, and had the pleasure of seeing the solemn lawyers in attendance hoot and holler with joy.[35] The story was too good to be left to the western Virginians, however, so storytellers from the mountain regions of North Carolina and Pennsylvania simply substituted their own neck of the woods for West Augusta. Ethnic communities, especially Scots-Irish but also German, also appropriated it for themselves. They insisted that they were the people whom Washington really trusted and among whom he would set his last standard.

The closest Washington ever came to suggesting that he might seek refuge in the West was in a letter of February 28, 1776, to Burwell Bassett in which he said, with apparent flippancy: "I thank you heartily for the attention you have kindly paid to my landed affairs on the Ohio, my interest in which I shall be more Careful of as in the worst event, they will serve for an Asylum."[36] But McDowell evidently borrowed Washington's alleged speech on this subject from Massachusetts minister William Gordon's 1788 history of the Revolutionary War. In it, Gordon claimed that the following conversation took place between Washington and Colonel Joseph Reed after the army reached Newark, New Jersey, in November 1776:

Washington: "Should we retreat to the back parts of Pennsylvania, will the Pennsylvanians support us?"

Reed: "If the lower counties are subdued and given up, the back counties will do the same."

Washington, touching a hand to his throat: "My neck does not feel as though it was made for a halter. We must retire to Augusta County in Virginia. Numbers will be obliged to repair to us for safety and we must try what we can do in carrying on a predatory war, and, if overpowered, we must cross the Alleghany Mountains."[37]

Washington made no such move, and there is no evidence from the period suggesting that he even considered it. For almost the entire time of Washington's stay at Newark, Reed was away in Burlington, New Jersey, and he never referred to any such conversation in any of his voluminous writings. Moreover, the source is dubious. Although Washington had reluctantly given Gordon temporary access to his papers, the minister simply copied large sections of his history from a contemporary British journalistic account of the war, the *Annual Register.* He also made up certain anecdotes in it to laud friends and demonize enemies. Gordon, said one contemporary, amounted to nothing more than a "mercenary scribbler who makes books with no other object than to gain a few pence." "If you take your ideas of the history of your country" from Gordon's book, John Adams warned Americans, "you will be deceived."[38] Most likely the quotation was a complete fabrication.

NOT JUST COMMUNITIES and regions claimed Washington as their own. Families also developed traditions—as in the cases of Darragh, Ross, and Honeyman—of an ancestor who had performed some important service for Washington. Just as large numbers of Americans claim descent from a Cherokee princess, many also claim descent from Washington's favorite bodyguard. If their stories are correct, the commander in chief must have stalked every battlefield surrounded by a throng of several thousand bodyguards jostling for position to stand at his right hand. Likewise, hordes of adoring children must have followed him everywhere. Literature and spoken tradition abounds with reminiscences of old men and women who had once received candy from Washington or bounced on his knee.

All of these personal, local, and popular stories and anecdotes, from the houses where Washington slept to the spies with whom he consorted, emerged from Americans' enduring desire to know Washington personally. Stone obelisks and statues, fawning paeans, and dry academic tomes told them nothing of the man. They wanted him as he lived and breathed; better, as one of themselves. Nobody wanted to hear that Washington *might have* done this or that, that he *might have* slept here, or that this piece of bric-a-brac *could have* belonged to him. They wanted stories. By the last quarter of the nineteenth century, as Americans looked back over one hundred years of history as readers, tourists, and participants in public celebrations, this need for a personal connection with Washington, the great Founder, had grown into a passionate craving.

CHAPTER 6

Washington Debunked

William E. Woodward was fed up with Wall Street, even though financially times were good. He was a banker in the Roaring Twenties, and his corporation was awash in cash. He didn't even need to exert himself. Every day he strolled to his office, signed a few papers, and went to play golf. Banking, he complained, "called for no creative energy. Nearly every problem that comes up in a bank is provided for by the law. No real thinking is required. When everybody in the bank's service gets familiar with the banking code and follows it there is really nothing for the leading officials of the bank to do." And though he sailed to and fro across New York City in a chauffeured limousine, indulging every whimsy, the apparent crass idiocy of consumer culture infuriated him. He had worked for years as an adman and seen the cynicism behind the pretense. Capitalism, he believed, had subjugated America to legions of tricksters, feeding the masses on illusion.[1]

George Washington bobbed along conspicuously in the consumerist tide. On a brief shopping trip in Manhattan, Woodward would have encountered the Founder peering out solemnly from cutlery, coin banks, pipes, pins, liquor flasks, trivets, watch fobs, ice cream molds, and every other imaginable place. Salesmen used Washington to hawk books, magazines, posters, cigars, apples, whiskey, batteries—again, everything imaginable. This close and growing association of Washington with American consumer culture affected Woodward far differently than the advertisers intended. For him, the omnipresence and artificiality of the Washington image conjured up associations of selfishness and greed and left him feeling disgusted rather than enticed. In time, as Woodward's anticonsumerism developed into a personal moral crusade, defacing that image took on the appearance of a sacred duty.

When a dispute arose one day with his board of directors, Woodward resolved not to give an inch. He didn't care if they fired him. And when their secretary came into his office, informing him that he was being asked to resign, Woodward burst into laughter. He was "through forever with loans and banks, and balance sheets and boards of directors." His wife, Helen, also took the news cheerfully. "I'm forty-six years old," William said at dinner that night. "What's cheerful about it?" "Why, my goodness," she replied, "now's your chance to write a book." And so he did.

Woodward decided to begin with fiction, and trolled about Paris and London looking for inspiration. One day, walking along a London pier and stewing about greed and the business world, he bought a copy of the *Times* from a newsboy. Looking inside, he read an article on how British soldiers had been deloused during World War I. He had been thinking of Henry Ford's use of the word *bunk*, or *bunkum*, to denote fraud and deceit. The connection was automatic. "If you could delouse a man," he thought, "you could also debunk him." Looking up over the ocean, he realized he had found a sense of literary purpose. His first novel would be titled *Bunk*, and he would become a debunker.

Bunk was published in 1923. It sold well, and Woodward wrote two more novels over the next two years in which he shredded the Wall Street tycoons and captains of industry. *Debunkery* became a household word, and publishers took note—his books paid. In 1926, publisher Horace Liveright contracted with Woodward for a $5,000 advance and 15 percent royalties on a new book. This time it would be nonfiction. Woodward had determined to take his debunker's hammer to that most cherished of American icons: George Washington. "I have a feeling," he wrote in his diary as the book came into print, "that I shall never live down my debunking reputation."

A few months later, after *George Washington: Image and Man* had circulated for a while and he had boosted sales with a book signing and radio tour, Woodward received an anonymous letter:

W. E. Woodward: "Halfway and Half Wit historian," as you were called before a prominent woman's club of a large city yesterday. This should be a yellow sheet instead of a pink one, because of all the yellow Americans you are the yellowest. How dare you speak on the radio about the Father of Our Country who wouldn't wipe his feet on you? . . . My aim is to kill your book. . . . I am looking for some friend who will assist me in buying as many copies of your book as possible to put in a bonfire, and in my will I shall set aside a sum for that purpose.

Woodward chuckled. "Thank you, Madam," he wrote in his autobiography. "I get fifteen per cent of the selling price of the life of Washington. It is a four-dollar book, and my profit is sixty cents. Why not buy a thousand of them for your bonfire?"[2]

WOODWARD DIDN'T JUST DEBUNK; he demolished. In his telling, Washington's family consisted of "sane and dull . . . excessively normal" people distinguished only by their "persistent mediocrity." George's father was a loutish glutton who died of overindulgence and gout, his mother a "hard, querulous" woman. They neglected their children, and George received a miserable education. He never learned how to spell properly. "He was never able to get the i's and the e's right in such words as ceiling," Woodward claimed; "he always wrote blew when he meant the color blue; lie was lye; and oil was oyl in his orthography." And though Washington loved numbers, it was only because he cherished "material possessions with a passionate intensity." Things, not ideas, interested him, and he had no use for books. He didn't even exhibit the dubious merits of a typical dumb jock. His muscles rippled, but out of proportion, and he stumbled through life with repulsively oversized hands and feet that constantly got in his way. He spent much of his time in the sickbed, groaning under the assaults of a series of ailments.[3]

Washington's public career was a sham. He accepted his first mission to the frontier out of "vanity" and fought the French and Indian War like an ignorant stripling. Later he supported the revolt against British rule out of greed, hoping that independence would enrich his estate. Hypocritically pretending not to seek command of the army, he secretly yearned for it as an opportunity for fame (an assertion still made by many historians today). He secured the position of commander in chief with the aid of an American aristocracy anxious to keep the people down. His refusal to accept pay was "snobbish," and he drove his men like a martinet. Only luck—and Nathanael Greene, who ran things at headquarters—saved Washington from disaster. Even his plan for the attack on Trenton was "hare-brained," and success a mere matter of chance.[4]

A "vast Milky Way of hazy thoughts" floated inside Washington's skull. Among politicians he was "grave, serious and bored," and as president he was a mere "figure-head." Alexander Hamilton governed the country while Washington calculated the income from his farms. Hard and cold, like the bankers of Woodward's day, Washington believed only in things he could see. Religion meant nothing to him except as a means of social control. He didn't shake hands, rarely laughed, and had little use for people except as pawns who could earn him money. He didn't drink liquor and rarely swore, not out of any sense of morality, but because he lacked imagination. Individualistic and wholly pragmatic, he thought like a cash register, adding up profits with no regard for others. His wartime experiences left him "grey inside" and utterly soulless, bereft of ideals and filled with contempt for human life. Washington didn't treat his slaves cruelly, but he valued them like horses, and judged the institution of slavery wholly on the basis of its economic value.

Woodward didn't much like Washington's contemporaries, either. "The Constitution," he said, "was planned like a coup d'etat" at the hands of a coterie of sleek, well-fed bankers. Colonials were squalid and greedy, or Puritanical hypocrites. Their arguments for revolution were childish and ridiculous. Thomas Paine was not only idiotic but sexually impotent. Lafayette was a "fool" with a deformed skull. Hamilton, a lifelong "careerist," was as "undemocratic as Mussolini" and an elitist snob. Even Martha—"a small, dumpy young woman, with dark eyes and a sharpish nose"—was "anti-democratic" and "anti-public." Her husband treated her as chattel, and she liked it that way. As for American Indians, they were sadists who taught their children to torture animals as training for the finer arts of inflicting pain on people.[5]

Woodward's real enemies were the hypocritically pious and patriotic old men who, he believed, ran things in the twentieth-century United States. He pricked Washington, their cherished icon, solely to embarrass them; hence his historical analysis had all the method and consistency of a swarm of angry bees. Woodward attacked myths cherished by Christians and patriots, but he accepted others without demur. And his research was selective. To prove Washington's intellectual degeneracy, for example, Woodward cited a few sloppy letters that he had composed as a youth, but he entirely disregarded the beautifully elucidated and carefully spelled missives that he wrote as an adult. Likewise, he made no attempt to plumb the nuances of Washington's military and political writings. His goal was to attack, not to understand.

Sloppy and strident though he was, Woodward set a trend. After 1926, debunkery exploded into popular literature. An article in the *Literary Digest*, nestled amid advertisements for Packer's Tar Soap, Phoenix Mutual Life Insurance, and Goodrich Zippers ladies' boots, told readers that the Founder had been a heavy drinker and party hound who despised women and built an empire on the corpses of the downtrodden. Like any Wall Street banker, he lived only for "business and amusement."[6] The *Nation* called Washington a cold, dull, and pompous leader who "had no conception of democracy, or of a society founded on anything but property."[7] Other journals leapt exultantly into the assault, slapping mud onto the Founder's marble statue until it stood hideously deformed— nothing from Mount Olympus, but a panting, gibbering monstrosity.

Debunkers inflicted extra pain where they struck unexpectedly. In 1926, a chapter of the Sons of the American Revolution invited Rupert Hughes, an accomplished writer and Hollywood director, to give an after-dinner speech about George Washington. He ruined his audience's digestion. Puffing out his chest, Hughes dubbed Washington a "great card-player, a distiller of whiskey, and a champion curser," who could dance for three hours without stopping. He never prayed, skipped out on communion, and regarded religion with contempt. The list went on. Enraged, the Sons denounced Hughes and booted him from their assembly, but he didn't mind—antagonizing people was his business.

Hughes stood short and stocky, but he was a big man

in Hollywood. Born in 1872 into a wealthy family, he had received a thorough education as a child and went to college at Yale, where he received a master's degree in English literature. Independent-minded, he refused to enter law school or pursue further graduate studies. Instead, he entered the New York literary scene in the 1890s, working as a cub reporter and a freelance poet. His gifts as a writer brought him immediate success. At first he wrote for risqué journals under pseudonyms, shocking readers with trashy stories and provocative editorials on women's rights, popular music, and religion, but more respectable journals soon took him on, including the *Saturday Evening Post*. He also wrote turgid romance novels for women and a number of plays, many of which were later adapted for silent movies. Following the money, Hughes moved to Hollywood and became a screenwriter, working for MGM and befriending stars such as Charles Chaplin. Making the most of precode Hollywood during World War I, he composed stories of German sexual atrocities with obvious relish, and battled advocates of censorship. Movies, he declared, were art and should stand inviolate from the attacks of canting parsons and namby-pamby old ladies who fainted at any references to pregnancy.

Hughes was a confirmed skeptic. As a child, he had been raised conventionally in a Protestant school and read his Bible every day, but at Yale he had taken on the motto "Question everything" and adopted Mark Twain as his literary idol. Emulating Twain, Hughes took to chomping cigars—although he never managed to replicate his hero's snow-white mustache and frizzy hair—and learned to mock organized religion. "Character," Hughes decided, "is so much more important than thou-shalt and thou-shalt-notting. Such pious, harmless people have such empty character and contribute so little beauty, grace or joy to the world, that they are really characterless."[8] In October 1924, Hughes officially came out of the closet with an essay for *Cosmopolitan* titled "Why I Quit Going to Church." God, he declared pretentiously, did not exist, and religion contributed nothing to a healthy society. Hughes expected to be attacked for his views, and he was. But in the tradition of the robust skepticism of his day, inspired by writers such as H. L. Mencken, Hughes derided his opponents with satire.

Like Woodward, Hughes knew that he could also tweak his enemies by attacking their icons.[9] But Hughes didn't fire from the hip. Since the turn of the twentieth century, he had studied Washington as a sort of hobby, building up a collection of books and manuscripts that had few rivals anywhere in the country. Hughes already knew his subject fairly well, therefore, when he began writing about him in the 1920s. His three-volume biography of Washington, published between 1926 and 1930, was well researched and documented, and relied heavily on a new edition of Washington's diaries that John Fitzpatrick had published in 1925. On the whole, though, Hughes's methods and conclusions did not differ much from Woodward's. His self-professed goal was to tear down the marble statue, and he went about it with a vengeance. "Say, did you read what Rupert Hughes dug up in George Washington's diary?" Will Rogers quipped. "I was so ashamed I sat up all night reading it."

Hughes's Washington was baptized to the tune of dance music by a drunken minister and grew up cowering under the iron rule of a "terrifyingly strict" mother, who smoked like a factory and burst out yelling without provocation. From her he inherited an argumentative nature and a "gift for bad spelling," but he also escaped through frenetic pleasure seeking, including dancing, fox hunting, gambling, and heavy drinking. Loutish and clumsy, Washington pursued every woman who passed his way, only to be jilted time and again. Sally Fairfax bedazzled him, but as she was strictly off-limits, Washington had to seek consolation in the chubby arms of Martha Dandridge Custis. Her wealth was only by-the-by. She was the only woman in Virginia who could be persuaded to marry such a pathetic creature as George Washington.

Marriage brought him consolation but not success. He failed as a farmer, leaving Mount Vernon choked with weeds and infested with rampaging squirrels. As a businessman, he amounted to nothing more than an honest sap. In politics he was a nonentity, routinely ignored or casually bullied by his more skilled colleagues. By 1775, he had accomplished "nothing at all," and as commander in chief of the Continental army, he gathered few laurels.[10] No wonder he had no sense of humor.

Hughes devoted much of his biography to debunkery, using Weems as a convenient straw man before moving on to other, more challenging targets. Among other things, Hughes dissected and discarded the stories that King Frederick the Great had expressed admiration for Washington and that Betsy Ross had sewn the first American flag. He took particular pleasure in destroying religious myths such as the prayer book, the Valley Forge prayer, and the Gano baptism. Like Woodward, however, Hughes selected his victims carefully, and he made no effort to criticize myths that supported the portrait of Washington that he labored to create. Thus Hughes repeated spurious anecdotes of Washington's infatuation with Mary Cary, the John Honeyman spy story, and the tale of drunk Hessian soldiers at the Battle of Trenton.[11] He also elaborated a few myths of his own. In speaking of the Battle of Trenton, Hughes repeated an old, entirely unsubstantiated anecdote of Washington taunting his favorite artilleryman, corpulent Colonel Henry Knox. On stepping into the boat that would carry him across the Delaware River, the story went, Washington had told Knox to shift his weight in the boat so he could have room to sit down. Hughes, deciding to elaborate a bit, claimed that in doing so Washington cracked a ribald joke about the size of Knox's bottom. Hughes had no evidence, aside from the usual anecdotal "tradition" that he was usually wont to deride—he just assumed that Washington, being a crude, foulmouthed yokel, would not have been able to resist the temptation to poke fun at poor Knox in front of his troops. Nineteenth-century censors, Hughes further assumed, probably knew the truth but had covered it up with their typical prudery.[12]

Hughes paraded his efforts to debunk Washington as if he had embarked on a kind of moral crusade. Weems, Sparks, Irving, and the like, he raged, had "helped to perpetuate as a devitalized deity one of the most eager, versatile, human men that ever lived." In telling the humble truth, Hughes revealed Washington as "real and lovable as well as admirable." "The man himself," he wrote, "is infinitely more appealing, pitiful, heartbroken, tragic, gay, witty, tender, gracious, tactful, fearless, ferocious, heroic, and, at his loftiest, sublime than the dull gray bore manufactured by stupid dullards, stodgy politicians and mongers of untruisms."[13] Hughes attracted attention not because he presented a balanced portrait of the

Founder, however, but because he defied convention in tearing Washington down.

Hughes's biography of Washington achieved tremendous commercial success. Probably relatively few people read it—Hughes's three volumes amounted, after all, to more than 2,000 pages of densely packed prose—but everyone knew, or thought they knew, what it said. It even became fashionable to own a copy, which served as a badge of independent thinking among members of the contemporary smart set. Patriotic critics raged and wondered what the country was coming to, but the debunkers' continued popularity ultimately left their opponents confounded. Hughes gave up on a projected fourth volume of the biography—the third volume had ended in 1781—but he continued to publish articles on Washington in the same debunking vein. By the 1930s, his views had become almost de rigueur. Hughes's own star faded somewhat after the late 1940s, when he actively cooperated with the House Un-American Activities Committee by telling them that the Screenwriters' Guild was "lousy with Communists," but his and Woodward's attempts to tear down the marble statue had achieved astonishing success. Washington would never be the same.[14]

WOODWARD AND HUGHES were creatures of their time every bit as much as Weems was of his. Prosperity, pleasure seeking, and iconoclasm all defined the 1920s. Gilded Age values, from laissez-faire economics to patriotic pomp and traditional Christianity, came under furious attack from nonconformists bent on ushering in a new age in Western civilization. For many, the Scopes "monkey trial" that ended in July 1925 symbolized the collision of nineteenth- and twentieth-century values. Clarence Darrow, the lawyer who defended schoolteacher John Scopes for teaching the theory of evolution in the classroom, was a founding member of the American Civil Liberties Union and stood at the forefront of the skeptical movement. Woodward, Hughes, and their fellow debunkers were skeptics, too, and devoted disproportionate energy to exploding myths of Washington's Christianity, branding all who disagreed as fundamentalist fanatics. "Well might the Father of His Country pray," declared debunker William Roscoe Thayer, "to be delivered from the parsons."[15]

Iconoclasts also assaulted the Washington who embodied the old-fashioned patriotism of John Philip Sousa and "The Star-Spangled Banner." Modernist poet William Carlos Williams, writing in 1925, called Washington "the Pap of Our Country," a false icon constructed to mislead Americans about the reality of their past. For Williams, America's true past was a story of oppression visited on downtrodden laborers and Native Americans by a wrathful coterie of Puritans and capitalists. Rather than count Washington among the oppressors, however, Williams portrayed him as another victim—a raw, passionate, noble creature of the frontier unwillingly corseted into the cruel mores of eighteenth-century high society. "Violently" attracted to young women, who feared his vital masculinity, Williams's Washington grew "curiously alive to the need of dainty waistcoats, lace and kid gloves, in which to cover that dangerous rudeness which he must have felt about himself."[16]

Williams's lustful Washington was, alas, stillborn, with no lasting impact on popular perceptions. The debunkers slashed through the Founding era like a raging whirlwind, carrying all the gaudy layers of nineteenth-century myth away with them, but on the whole they left a barren dust bowl behind. Though they were victorious in a sense, their impact was wholly negative. As the wild outrage that greeted its first appearance on the scene faded, debunking became commonplace, and ultimately passed out of style—if only because little remained to debunk.[17]

By the time of the Great Depression the mythical Washington had fallen into sad disarray, an object of mockery rather than adulation. Artist Grant Wood, best known for his 1930 painting *American Gothic*, satirized the Washington legend in two paintings, *Daughters of Revolution* (1932) and *Parson Weems's Fable* (1939). The former depicted three superannuated DAR ladies enjoying tea in front of Emanuel Leutze's famous— and by this time popularly derided—painting of Washington standing in a boat crossing the Delaware. Wood's placement of the painting graphically emphasized Washington's splayed legs with a hint of obscenity that called to mind Rupert Hughes's story of the commander in chief's coarse taunt of Henry Knox. The latter painting showed a smirking Parson Weems pulling back the curtain on an image of his famous story of Washington chopping down the cherry tree—absurdly displaying the Founder with a child's body and an old man's head.[18]

Myths maintained currency only so long as they showed Washington in a ridiculous light. One of the most popular had Alexander Hamilton daring Gouverneur Morris to pat Washington on the shoulder and say, "My dear General, how happy I am to see you look so well," in return for a free dinner and a bottle of wine. Morris did so, whereupon Washington stepped violently away from his friendly hand and fixed him with an apoplectic stare. A terrified Morris later confessed to Hamilton that he would not repeat the experiment for a thousand dinners.[19] *George Washington Slept Here*, a 1942 movie starring Jack Benny and Ann Sheridan, presented a mocking send-up of the historic homes phenomenon, which few people took seriously anymore. Ann purchases an old Pennsylvania farmhouse in which Washington supposedly slept, but she and Jack get more than they bargained for as the dilapidated old building slowly collapses around them.

Biographers and historians writing in the wake of the debunking firestorm conceived Washington with ultracautious realism. John C. Fitzpatrick, a quietly obscure scholar and Washington devotee who served as assistant chief of the Manuscript Division at the Library of Congress from 1902 to 1928, typified this trend. His 1925 publication of Washington's diaries, which had in part inspired the debunkers, was followed by the publication, from 1931 to 1940, of the monumental thirty-seven-volume edition of the *Writings of Washington* under the auspices of the Washington Bicentennial Commission. Fitzpatrick believed in facts and nothing but. "There has been a large amount of romancing about Washington," he wrote, "romancing being a much simpler, easier and speedier way of writing his life than assimilating the full truth by laborious research among an enormous collection of manuscripts."[20] His *Writings of Washington* reflected this approach, adhering stolidly to the text of the original letters with little of the jazzing up practiced in an earlier era by Jared Sparks.

In attempting to translate his research into a viable biography of Washington, Fitzpatrick failed miserably. "Everything for which documentary proof does not exist may be discarded without regret," he wrote in the preface to his book *George Washington Himself* (1930), "for the provable facts that remain support a life and character more than satisfactory to the most ardent admirer and more than sufficient to suppress the vain activities of the most captious critic."[21] Yet while no one could criticize Fitzpatrick's research, his Washington appeared lifeless as a mummy, true to the documents but devoid of soul and personality. Subsequent attempts by other authors, such as Grant Ritter's *Washington as a Business Man* (1931), impressed only insofar as they "dared to be deadly dull."[22] They scrupulously avoided mythmaking but cringed lest a hint of speculation for the purpose of adding color expose them to debunkers' steely knives.

Even the Washington bicentennial of 1932 fell flat, though not for lack of effort. In preparation, President Herbert Hoover appointed flamboyant congressman Sol Bloom to head the Bicentennial Commission. Hyperactively energetic and a natural showman, Bloom subjected the country—and the world—to a barrage of Washington mania, erecting busts and statues as far afield as Germany, Japan, Indochina, and Mexico; organizing public events, radio shows, and patriotic concerts; naming streets and buildings after Washington, and so on. He launched a campaign to bring Washington into American classrooms, not by way of Parson Weems's fables, but by pasting his image above every blackboard. Based on the Houdon bust that Washington had modeled for in 1785, it would be, unlike its nineteenth-century predecessors, unimpeachably authentic.

"You made the whole country Washington conscious," Will Rogers told Bloom. "We had just pictured him as a man standing up in a boat when he ought to be sitting down." But all of the fanfare amounted, as cultural historian Karal Ann Marling described it, to a strangely "austere hoopla." There were trinkets, masquerade balls, and kitsch aplenty, but unlike in 1876, Americans engaged in next to no mythmaking. To the contrary, the commemorations featured a good deal of self-congratulatory myth busting. Bloom's official pamphlet for the celebration contained a series of questions and answers about Washington that directly condemned a number of nineteenth-century myths and images, including Leutze's painting of Washington crossing the Delaware. "We need no attempt at a canonization of George Washington," President Hoover declared.[23] Neither idolized nor humanized, the Founder dissolved into intangibility.

THE AGE OF MYTH did not go down without a fight. Here and there the old stories kept popping through, even in official venues, as with the commemorative postage stamp showing Washington praying in the snow. And teachers and children struggled to give up on Weems. As a satirist wrote at the time:

> Let others echo Rupert Hughes
> And mix up motes and beams—
> The anecdotes that I peruse
> Were told by Parson Weems.
>
> Above iconoclastic vies
> That little hatchet gleams!
> "I cannot tell a lie," I choose
> The Washington of Weems.[24]

Amid the cherry tree and wooden teeth, however, teachers mixed a hodgepodge of debunkery—telling their students, for example (much to their glee), that Washington didn't know how to spell. Such mockery helped to alleviate fatigue caused by the usual rote—what later generations would call "making history fun."

Divested of his vital humanity and detached from the patriotic pantheon, Washington the symbol ironically became easier to manipulate. As he meant nothing, so he could mean anything. In the 1930s, radicals routinely integrated Washington's portrait into their own imagery. At a German-American Bund rally at New York's Madison Square Garden in 1939, a thirty-foot-tall portrait of Washington glowered out over a sea of swastikas. Communists depicted him as the radical head of an army of proletarians rising against British oppression. However he appeared, Washington remained empty, superficial, and thoroughly uninteresting. Maxwell Anderson's 1934 play *Valley Forge*, which depicted a remarkably wooden commander in chief, ran into trouble on the way to Hollywood. Directors Frank Capra and John Ford purchased the movie rights in 1937 but could not convince their financial backers to climb on board. "Who the hell's interested in George Washington?" one of them yelled at Capra. "That's dead fish, nobody's interested in the American Revolution."[25]

World War II generated the inevitable comparisons between the GIs and their predecessors in the Continental army, but failed to spur renewed interest in George Washington. As a symbol, he seemed lusterless and uninspiring; especially at a time when living figures such as FDR and Churchill loomed so much larger than life. He appeared only rarely on posters and other patriotic paraphernalia, and no new myths of his bravery and noble deeds emerged to embolden the troops. This state of affairs could not last forever, however. Washington had become too ingrained in American history and self-identity to disappear permanently from popular culture. Somewhere, deep below the surface, he slept, waiting for the magician who would conjure him back to life.

CHAPTER 7

The Indispensable Man

HOLLYWOOD GAVE WASHINGTON HIS FIRST—and as it turned out, his only—chance on the big screen in 1951, in a movie titled *When the Redskins Rode*. Shot in an antiquated process called Supercinecolor, it starred B-movie stalwart James Seay as young Colonel George Washington and Jon Hall, a former leading man well past his prime, in the romantic lead role as Delaware Indian prince Hannoc. Seay had once aimed for stardom in Hollywood, but his weak, undistinguished facial features put the kibosh on that. Instead, producers typecast him in Cold War sci-fi movies as the expendable army guy who always gets killed. This proclivity for playing nonentities made Seay a natural for the role of George Washington.

The story begins in 1753, with Washington and his frontiersman pal Christopher Gist hanging out with Hannoc in

Williamsburg, Virginia. Just for kicks, Washington and Gist have snatched Hannoc out of the wilderness and taught him to dress and behave like a European. This doesn't tax anyone too severely, especially since Hall, the actor playing Hannoc, looks more like a middle-aged Italian than a young Indian. Worried by this growing camaraderie, the French—who stand in for the Russkies in this Cold War epic—nefariously attempt to subvert Hannoc by sending young Elizabeth Leeds to seduce him. She succeeds, and Hannoc falls in love.

The more business-minded Washington meanwhile leads an intrepid band of rangers to confront the French at their frontier outpost, Fort LeBoeuf. This part of the script is based on real events—sort of—but the sets are a bit off. In the winter of 1753–54, Washington trekked to the fort through the snow-choked primeval forests and mountains of western Pennsylvania, interacting and sometimes fighting with tribes of eastern woodland Indians. In the movie, he approaches the fort through terrain straight out of a B-movie western, dodging tumbleweeds and sagebrush, enduring searing desert heat, and battling bands of screaming Apaches. Wicked Lizzy Leeds makes his job harder by tipping off the French, who team up with some of Geronimo's boys and try to ambush George and his hearty band in camp. Fortunately, Hannoc is there, and after a quick sniff of the air he warns his friends, foiling the attack at the last moment.

Reaching the fort—a western stockade probably used as an outpost by some of Custer's 7th U.S. Cavalry—Washington delivers his ultimatum to the French: get out of the Ohio country or else! Miffed, the sneaky French commandant claps the upstart Virginians in prison, whereupon Washington nonchalantly shoots his way out and ignites the powder magazine to blow up the fort. On the way back to Virginia, Washington's gang wrestles with Indians who drop out of trees like overripe apples, and chase elusive blue-coated Frenchmen who scamper randomly through the underbrush. Occasionally they pause to watch a passing boat full of Frenchmen overturn and sink in river rapids.

Amid all this frenetic action, Hannoc catches a French spy embracing Lizzy Leeds and beats him up. His long-suffering former girlfriend—an Indian, and thus more racially compatible by 1950s standards—then strangles the French seductress. Hannoc's reunion with his old flame and the disposal of the French spies comes just in time, for Washington and Gist have gotten themselves in another jam, this time at Fort Necessity—actually Fort LeBoeuf with a minor makeover. Hostile Indians swarm over the walls of the stockade and fire flaming arrows while French officers chuckle menacingly and the sycophant Gist gasps, "George, I don't think we can hold out much longer!" Just as they are about to surrender, Hannoc and his good Indian buddies ride to the rescue, beat off the bad Indians, and save the day. The Battle of Fort Necessity has ended in victory! Hannoc and his new girl embrace, Washington and Gist guffaw and slap backs, and the scene fades to closing credits.

When the Redskins Rode remains the only big-screen movie ever to feature George Washington in anything more than a minor role. During the early silent-movie era, Washington strutted on-screen in a variety of insignificant one-reelers, such as *How Mrs. Murray Saved the American Army* (1911), and during World War I he appeared in a number of patriotic shorts. During the 1920s and 1930s, however, Washington all but disappeared from the silver screen. British-born character actor Alan Mowbray played him several times, most notably in the 1931 biopic *Alexander Hamilton*, but always in peripheral roles. During World War II, Washington turned up from time to time as a patriotic symbol, like the flag, but never as a character. Most often he appeared in comedies, usually as a ghost or as a character in somebody's wacky dream.

After *When the Redskins Rode*, as the television era gathered momentum in the 1950s, Washington gained occasional spots in shows such as *You Are There*, hosted by Walter Cronkite, the *Hallmark Hall of Fame*, and the *NBC Saturday Showcase*. Most of these were historical docudramas focused on an event, such as the Battle of Trenton, rather than on Washington. He also appeared on the kids' show *Captain Z-Ro* and an episode of *The Phil Silvers Show*. Probably his biggest part in the 1960s— aside from his zany supernatural antics in *One Step Beyond*— was as an empty costume in a 1964 episode of *The Munsters*. By then, Washington's already meager star power had faded away to zilch.

Washington's inability to hit the big time in an increasingly media-driven culture reflected his ongoing image problem. By the middle of the twentieth century, he had become a symbol as colorless and two-dimensional as a washed-out old flag. To some extent this resulted from overexposure, as if the grand old man had come down with a hangover after the decades of toasts that Americans had drunk to his honor. "His popularity," wrote Karal Ann Marling, "had finally blunted all sense of what that large and lonely figure really stood for. . . . Washington had come to be a bore."[1]

Americans hadn't really lost interest in Washington. His image still hovered everywhere, from school classrooms and history books to newspapers and advertising. But the storytelling had ended. In the nineteenth century, Parson Weems and his followers had gathered, embellished, and disseminated rich currents of folklore concerning the Founder. Though false—often ridiculously so—their stories had lent to Washington a degree of vibrancy and three-dimensionality that he might otherwise have lost, making him a man for all people and occasions. In exploding this gaudy fairy world in the 1920s, Woodward, Hughes, and their fellow debunkers had taken the fun out of Washington and transformed him into a plate of cold fish.

The scientific brutality with which the debunkers dissected earlier mythmakers left behind a legacy of fear. Twentieth-century Washington biographers trod timidly, probing for land mines in realms where their nineteenth-century forbears had swung forward with a devil-may-care step. Teachers and textbook writers, once inspired by Weems into weaving pious but often deliciously imaginative stories around the country's Founder, now subjected their pupils to dreary rote. The baby boom generation probably learned the facts of the Founder's life more accurately than ever before. Without the glue of imagination and inspiration, however, their lessons lacked staying power, falling away the moment that the children walked out the classroom door. As the baby boomers grew to maturity during the political and social turmoil of the 1960s, Washington seemed as irrelevant as the ideals for which he had once stood. Yet even as America embarked upon a new, cynical age, relief loomed on the horizon.

A new generation of showmen was on the way.

*   *   *

JAMES THOMAS FLEXNER was born in 1908 to a prominent Manhattan family. His father, Simon Flexner, worked as a research physician and devoted his life to seeking a cure for infantile paralysis. His mother, Helen Thomas Flexner, was a progressive-thinking modern woman who moved in upper-crust New York literary circles. James Flexner struggled with dyslexia throughout childhood, but he refused to let it defeat him. Indeed, he had no choice. His mother had marked him out since birth as the writer of the family, and she pressed him mercilessly to succeed. One day, sitting in Central Park pondering a Peter Rabbit book by Beatrix Potter, inspiration struck, and young James Flexner suddenly found himself reading. His appetite for books became insatiable, and childish stories and poems poured in torrents from his pen. The realization brought him no rest, however. Dyslexia remained a constant nemesis, and schoolyard bullying left him frightened and insecure, but his mother forced him to keep pushing forward. Composition as a means of expression was all very well, she told him, but eventually he must put aside childish things and set his sights on becoming a professional writer.

This constant pressure to succeed contributed to the anxiety attacks that plagued Flexner throughout his life and sometimes left him trembling on the verge of madness.[2] Fortunately, he possessed both creative energy and talent in abundance. Entering Harvard at age seventeen, he astounded his professors by acing tests and demonstrating a natural talent for resplendent prose. A perceptive observer, he watchfully noted the various quirks and traits of the larger-than-life literary characters that surrounded his mother, and integrated their personalities into the imaginary communities of his writings. Graduating summa cum laude, Flexner felt confident enough to apply his writing skills immediately, and turned down graduate school in favor of taking a spot as a cub reporter with the *New York Herald Tribune*.[3] The job didn't lead to the literary fame he expected, but he kept plugging away at his writing, and after a short interval he took up a minor bureaucratic position with the city government.

Flexner completed his first major literary piece, a novel, while holding this government position, and he hoped that it would set him firmly on the road to literary fame. Alas, every publisher returned a rejection. The failure of this first literary venture crushed Flexner, seeming as it did to "mark a betrayal of my family inheritance and expectations, and ultimate failure in my lifelong ambition."[4] His anxiety attacks returned with redoubled force, leading to a nervous breakdown and a stay in the hospital. Worse, he developed a severe and complete case of writer's block. As with his childhood dyslexia, the solution to Flexner's dilemma came in a sudden burst of inspiration. His compositions, he had to admit, had never stood out for plotting or imaginative conceptualization. In one area, though, he stood out above all others: his almost uncanny knack for characterization. He made people come alive. The answer, then, seemed obvious. No longer would Flexner attempt to establish himself as a novelist, playwright, or poet. He would become a biographer.

When he made this decision, Flexner's writer's block disappeared. In 1937, he published his first book, *Doctors on Horseback: Pioneers in American Medicine*, a collection of character sketches that included his father. It was a smashing success. Emboldened, he exultantly determined to make *Doctors on Horseback* the "first in a series that would blaze trails in one neglected field after another."[5] Beginning with *America's Old Masters: First Artists of the New World* (1939), he embarked on a series of popular biographies of American artists, doctors, and scientists that opened up new vistas on long-overlooked corners of the country's past. They proved wildly popular, and he quit his government post to take up writing full-time. His mother's ambitions for him finally seemed fulfilled.

Success could not temper Flexner's nagging insecurities, however, and even as he grew in popularity he began looking for enemies in the woodwork. Though he boasted frequently of his accomplishments at Harvard, he remained acutely conscious of the fact that he had never received formal training as a historian. And though academic reviews of his books had been almost uniformly positive, he could not rid himself of the imaginary bogey of academic disapproval. The halls of higher learning, he grew increasingly certain, overflowed with balefully gazing, troglodyte hordes of tenure-seeking academics who eagerly awaited opportunities to curry favor with their colleagues by rending him to bits. After the publication of *America's Old Masters*, his imagination conjured phantom cohorts of "genealogists and antiquarians obscurely proceeding down their restricted paths . . . sharpening their pencils for the kill." Only the timely endorsement of his book by a prominent art authority saved Flexner, as he believed, from destruction.

This lurking academic menace did not entirely cow Flexner. Instead, he adopted the persona of a maverick, telling himself that he would boldly bring history to the American people despite the scholars' envious cries of "heresy, presumption, and insanity."[6] Flexner did not pretend to any false modesty. In *America's Old Masters* and its successors, he swore, he had single-handedly established American artists in the international pantheon, and he openly reveled in positive reviews, awards, and royalty checks. When America entered World War II, Flexner adroitly avoided military service by securing testimonials from some of the most prominent Freudian psychiatrists in the country, getting one of them to write to the draft board that he must be removed from consideration because of "psyasthenic obsessive fears which hamper him greatly in the ordinary moves of practical life: the difficulty of breaking his routine, inability to go to theatres, difficulty of sleep, and special gastrointestinal involvements." The board's subsequent decision to declare him 4-F left Flexner "greatly relieved," but he took pleasure in the knowledge that his books, issued to the troops in armed service editions, had been "entrusted with sustaining morale in our own fighting forces." "There was no reason," he concluded, "for me to skulk when women stopped me in the street to ask why I was not in uniform."[7]

Pushing on, Flexner decided that the time had come for him to pass beyond medicine and art and take on some of the biggest and most important figures in American history. Royalty receipts for his art books had anyway begun to decline as the novelty wore off. At first Flexner set his mind to one of the most dramatic moments in American history: Benedict Arnold's treason and attempted betrayal of West Point during the Revolutionary War. Replete with larger-than-life figures, the subject seemed ready-made for his pen. Just as Flexner prepared to begin writing, however, someone cut in line in front of him. The administrators of the Clements Library, which held the most important primary documents relating to Arnold's treason under lock and key, commissioned biographer Carl Van Doren to write a history of the event, and granted him exclusive access to their holdings. Flexner fumed. Van Doren, a handsome and urbane literary genius who had won the Pulitzer Prize in 1938 for his biography of Benjamin Franklin, was, Flexner opined, a "pompous ass" who deserved no part of his success.

Van Doren wrote quickly, and when his book *The Secret History of the American Revolution* hit the shelves in 1941, Flexner snatched up a copy and perused it with a jaundiced eye. He found it both too short and poorly written. Van Doren, he decided, "cluttered emotional effect with detail following more detail, equally weighted." Flexner knew he could do better, sensing an "epic, sensational story" whose heroes and villains were well-nigh "Wagnerian" in quality. A number of lingering art book projects hindered his research for several years, but in 1953 Flexner published his own account of the treason, *The Traitor and the Spy*.[8] Reviewers hailed it as one of the greatest history books of the century, and even academics fell into line. In revealing the story behind Arnold's treason, proclaimed the *New York Times Book Review*, Flexner had demonstrated a "literary power and intensity" rarely seen before.

With Flexner's return to the ranks of bestselling authors, publishers took note. In *The Traitor and the Spy*, Flexner had shown that he belonged in the top rank of American biographers. He needed only a subject suited to his genius. In 1961, representatives of the publishing house Little, Brown approached Flexner and suggested that he write a biography of America's greatest hero, George Washington. Who better than Flexner, they said, to rescue Washington from decades of exile and return him to the people?

As a biographer, and moreover one who prided himself

on exploring new ground and reviving neglected topics, breathing life into the desiccated Founder seemed a noble and possibly extremely profitable objective. But Flexner never undertook anything lightly. Any book he wrote must not be just one of many on the subject, or even the best of its time, but definitive, never to be surpassed. The recent completion of a monumental seven-volume biography of Washington by Douglas Southall Freeman made Flexner's challenge all the greater. It "frowned down," as Flexner put it, upon every prospective Washington biographer like a frosty mountain range.[9]

Born in 1886 in Lynchburg, Virginia, Freeman took his southern heritage with his mother's milk, and idolized his father, a battle-tested Confederate veteran. He was a shy, studious, and devoutly religious lad. Like Flexner, Freeman wanted to become a writer, and he made some clumsy ventures into romantic fiction, but unlike Flexner, he also aspired to be a scholar. After going to Richmond College, Freeman studied history for four years at Johns Hopkins University and received his Ph.D. in 1908. His grades were superb, but his writing left something to be desired. "Freeman," a professor rebuked him after slogging through a particularly turgid paper, "the research in this paper is excellent, indeed exceptionable. But you will never make a writer."[10]

Freeman's subsequent schooling as a journalist helped to lighten his writing style. After graduating from Johns Hopkins, he went to work for the *Richmond Times-Dispatch*, and in 1915 he became editor of the *Richmond News Leader*. As scholar and journalist, his approach to research and writing remained the same as it had always been. Newspaper editors, he opined, must never try to manipulate emotions, but "keep the mind of the crowd from becoming the mind of the mob . . . keep the instincts from overwhelming the sentiments, the reason, and the emotions of the people."[11] The historian must likewise avoid emotions and devote himself to dispassionate, scientific research: "fidelity to facts, measured interpretation, and economy of expression."[12] Freeman applied these standards simultaneously in his editorship of the *Richmond News Leader* and in his scholarly writing. He spent twenty years researching and writing a biography of his idol, Robert E. Lee, which was published in four volumes in 1934–35, and a subsequent three-volume work, *Lee's Lieutenants*, which came out in 1942–44.

Freeman was already a nationally famous historian and biographer by the time he began working on his biography of George Washington in November 1944. Funded handsomely by the Carnegie Corporation, he hired a team of researchers to help him in his work. Freeman was no sluggard, however, and instead of leaning on his researchers to do the heavy lifting, he devoted every speck of energy left over from his journalism to this new work. From the start, he professed the same objectives as every Washington biographer before him. "Washington did not himself climb up on a marble pedestal, strike a pose and stay there," he told reporters from *Time* magazine. "What we're going to do, please God, is to make him a human being. The great big thing stamped across that man is character."[13]

Freeman saw in George Washington an intensely ambitious and emotional man who struggled throughout his life to maintain self-control and labored to greatness through a sea of missteps and mistakes. In bringing out the real man, Freeman refused to step beyond his scholarly standards or

employ literary shortcuts in favor of evocative characterization. Critics therefore praised his work as a piece of scholarship but complained about the "plodding . . . portentous"
narrative overladen with "often inconsequential detail [so
that] even the student nods."[14] And it was long—very long.
From 1948 to 1953, Freeman completed six doorstop-sized
volumes, yet reached only into Washington's first presidential
administration.

Confident in the integrity of his methods, Freeman
shrugged off the critics. His passion for history and humble
belief in the pursuit of truth acted as his armor. "Everyman
must have his work," he wrote, "and that is mine—to labour
earnestly, to labour honestly, and bring out something that
may be worth men's whiles to read, something that in times
to come, may be taken as final—a word said on a subject, and
a word apropos. I know that means a long time of labour, a
long line of years with but slight remuneration. But for my
part, I am willing to starve—as the saying goes—for twenty
years, if at the end of that time it can be honestly said that I
have done a good piece of work."[15] And good it was. Freeman's *George Washington* remains probably the most scholarly
book ever written on its subject, but it was the kind of book
that people bought and never read.

Flexner sensed this weakness. Freeman, he noted, had
given all the details of Washington's life but skimped on
"character delineation and evocative presentation."[16] He didn't
much like Freeman as a person, either. Lanky and balding,
with spectacles that sat perched upon an aquiline nose, the
chain-smoking Freeman was a political and economic conservative and a consummate gentleman. He spoke slowly, with
easy southern grace, and was quick to self-deprecate. Flexner,

by contrast, was a short, hyperkinetic redhead, a moderate leftist, and a Yankee born and bred. He was also highly competitive and could not conceive of Freeman's humility as anything other than hypocrisy. During the early 1950s, while Flexner was deep in writing *The Traitor and the Spy*, Freeman called him up and gently asked if he might be willing to share some tidbits of information he had dug up, from one scholar to another. Astonished at such gall, Flexner for a moment considered firing back "with the New York colloquialism based on the rivalry of two department stores: 'Does Macy's tell Gimbels'?' " Instead he just told Freeman that he would save his discoveries for his own book.[17]

Freeman died in 1953, leaving the seventh and final volume of his biography of Washington to be finished from his notes by his researchers in 1957. His work remained on the scene, however, seeming to crowd out all potential competition, if only by virtue of its bulk. If dry, it was free of myth and impossible to debunk. It said everything, it seemed, that could possibly be said of Washington. But the indomitable Flexner did not have it in his "nature to be frightened by competition." Accepting Little, Brown's offer, he headed to the New York Public Library's card catalog to survey everything that had been written about Washington over the past 160 years. He found more than 3,000 cards but refused to be intimidated. Instead, Flexner decided that the only way to deal with this mass would be to throw it all out. Declaring that he would "conquer by my own strength alone," Flexner set Freeman's seven-volume biography on his shelf next to Fitzpatrick's edition of Washington's writings, reserved desks at the New York Public Library and at Mount Vernon, and set out to write a biography essentially from scratch, paying no heed—or so he claimed—to any other writers who had gone before him.[18]

For all his talk of taking the wider view and writing about Washington only from the hundreds of thousands of letters that constituted his original correspondence, Flexner made no pretence of Freeman-style painstaking research. This would be no work of twenty or thirty years. He meant to write a compelling story, and he intended for people to read it. After some teaser installments in *American Heritage* magazine, the first volume of Flexner's biography appeared in 1965, the second in 1968, the third in 1970, and the fourth and final volume in 1972. This quick pace fed off the immense popularity of volume one and kept the public eager and ready for more.

Flexner's stated goal echoed Freeman's, and for that matter just about every other Washington biographer for the past hundred years: he would make the Founder human. Citing Sigmund Freud on the first page of his introduction to the first volume—and possibly drawing on lessons learned from his own therapy—Flexner declared that Americans had transformed Washington into a collective "infantile phantasy," modeling him after their own fathers as an impersonal, featureless marble statue. Flexner would dismantle that statue and reintroduce Washington to the United States as a genuine human being. His portrait was compelling. Awkward and vain as a youth, Washington struggled through a series of personal and military mistakes and a wrenching "dark love" for Sally Fairfax to claw his way to glory. His greatness as a general and president derived not from any infallible attributes but from perseverance, self-confidence, an ability to learn from mistakes, and a will to succeed. He was not the smartest man in America, or even the strongest or bravest. Instead, he displayed in aggregate just the right series of qualities that his country needed at the time. Washington, according to a phrase that Flexner brilliantly coined, was America's "indispensable man."

This astute assessment was not wholly original—Flexner borrowed from Freeman more than he was ever willing to admit—but wonderfully concise and evocative. It not only encapsulated Washington's greatness in a way that ordinary people could understand but also influenced generations of scholars. Where Flexner really broke from his predecessors, however, was in the technique he used to humanize his subject. In years past, Washington biographers had followed in Parson Weems's footsteps, drawing on anecdotes from myth and folklore to make their subject more real and interesting. The debunkers had discredited that approach after the 1920s and caused subsequent Washington biographers to avoid adding the least jab of color that did not jibe with established facts. Flexner, consummate writer that he was, demonstrated that a popular biography could avoid both extremes and humanize Washington by virtue of one vital quality: imaginative writing.

Flexner began with basic facts. These had become readily available, thanks to Fitzpatrick and others, through the wealth of Washington's writings, including his diaries, now available to the public. Where Freeman and other "scientific" historians had been content to rely on these to construct an authentic if somewhat humdrum series of events, Flexner applied his imagination to elucidate on these facts and create vivid scenes and flesh-and-blood characters. Thus, starting from a document describing the bare-bones facts of a certain event, Flexner added the facial expressions, bodily gestures, figures of speech, and private thoughts of Washington and all the other dramatis personae, setting it all against the backdrop of a vividly described albeit largely imaginary physical scene. In essence, he wrote a historical novel based on fact, but without admitting it as such. Instead, Flexner duly cited the authentic, if sparse, original sources on which he based his dramatic scenes. Where this seemed too glaringly inadequate, he, like nineteenth-century mythmakers, fell back on the old standby phrases: unspecified "copious evidence" and "unimpeachable sources."

Many of Flexner's imaginative meanderings were harmless if not always entirely plausible. He described Washington—entirely without evidence—as being "relieved" not to be sent off to sea as a young man, as being so entranced with the beauty of the western frontier that he surrendered a part of his heart to it, and as worrying fretfully as he listened to the tubercular cough of his half brother Lawrence Washington.[19] Other concoctions, equally unfounded, blurred the boundaries of biography and fiction. In describing the events of 1753–54, when Washington trekked the snowy woods of western Pennsylvania with the frontiersman Christopher Gist, Flexner spun out a dramatic fantasy from documents that noted nothing more than their temporary separation with a promise to meet again in the woods farther ahead:

> As Washington moved alone through the lethal cold, he listened for a nearby rustle that would mean danger for him, for a distant shot might mean the death of Gist. Darkness poured down. Surely his heart pounded in his breast as he neared the trysting place. Yes, there was a blacker shadow! Yes, his friend was there![20]

Further on, Flexner described Washington camping in the woods with his troops before the battle of Fort Necessity. Primary sources—accurate but colorless—indicated that Washington's men raised an alarm during the night and that six of them disappeared. To Flexner, these bare facts suggested a much more exciting scene:

> In the middle of the night, as Washington dozed to whippoorwill and wolf howl, shots! The sentries had fired! He rushed to them: they had seen shadowy figures out there in the dark. Washington's men were now all up and around him under arms. He spaced them behind the ramparts, and everyone stared over, everyone listened. Nothing to see; wolf howl, whippoorwill, and wind in the trees. Finally, dawn. No bodies, upright or prone, became visible in the cleared meadows, but six of Washington's soldiers proved to be missing. It must have been these deserters who triggered the alarm.[21]

Flexner's lack of compunction in applying these literary devices stemmed in part from his confidence in himself as a psychologist. He believed he had gotten the measure of his subject and could therefore safely present his speculations about Washington's thoughts and feelings as if they were incontrovertible facts. He was particularly interested in the Sally Fairfax legend for what it seemed to say about Washington's passionate personality. Describing Washington's return from the frontier after the disastrous Battle of the Monongahela in 1755, Flexner used a few letters mentioning only that Washington had been feeling ill, and that he had returned home to Mount Vernon, to spin a neat little romantic fantasy. Reeling with illness and fatigue, Washington staggered through the front door at Mount Vernon, lurched up the stairs, and "with a final push of dying energy . . . made his way upstairs to fall on his bed."[22] A moment later a knock on the door announced a letter from Sally, and his spirits immediately revived. In Flexner's telling, Sally was indeed the true love of Washington's life, his marriage to Martha a matter of convenience that allowed him a form of escape from his unrequitable passion.

Flexner deftly avoided repeating past myths and legends. He ignored Betsy Ross, John Honeyman, and Washington as the man who could have been king. He also explored some areas of Washington's life that scholars had been reluctant to plumb, such as slavery, and he presented a largely balanced and accurate assessment of the Founder's religious beliefs. Yet Flexner also created myths of his own. To take one of numerous examples, in depicting Washington during the siege of Boston in the winter of 1775–76, Flexner elaborated from a primary source mentioning that Washington once went to check the harbor ice to state that "when morning came, he would go out to the bay and jump up and down on the ice in the harbor. It was strong enough to carry his army all the way to the British." David McCullough repeated this image—entirely the product of Flexner's imagination—in his book *1776*, and it was later picked up by a television documentary.[23] More perniciously, Flexner's negative view of Martha Washington, borrowed in part from debunkers such as Rupert Hughes—whom he consulted extensively despite his pronounced disavowal of secondary sources—poisoned popular perceptions of the Founder's wife well into the twenty-first century.

*   *   *

FLEXNER'S BIOGRAPHY OF WASHINGTON far outsold anything written about the first president since Mason Locke Weems. Reviews were almost uniformly positive, and volume four even won a special Pulitzer citation. Mr. Flexner "brought the hero down from Olympus," declared Thomas Lask in the *New York Times*, "to where we can see him whole and see him plain."[24] Of all these Flexner was immensely proud, yet he could not resist continuing to play the maverick. Everywhere, he believed, academies belched forth unseen enemies who clutched at his lapels and demanded to see his nonexistent professional credentials. "Dry-as-dust scholars," "Ph.D. candidates and buckers for tenure," and "associate professors in jerkwater colleges," he growled, had cast him under intense "hostile scrutiny" and malevolently brandished "envenomed darts," but his chin remained upturned in defiance. "Despite their best efforts," he crowed, "they have been able to find only a thin scattering of factual errors, mostly misspellings."[25] Even the establishment in 1968 of a new, massive project at the University of Virginia—the Papers of George Washington, which would transcribe and publish every known letter to and from Washington, completely dwarfing the Fitzpatrick edition on which Flexner had relied—left him unruffled. "I was not frightened by this brontosaurus snuffling at my tail," he wrote. The editors of this new project were wasting their time and might as well close up shop, Flexner believed. He had already discovered everything of any possible value, and his volumes would carry all competition before them, into perpetuity:

The vast majority of the letters addressed to Washington would be of value only to students of the writers, and I was confident that almost all papers directly of importance to the study of Washington had already come, one way or another, into my ken. It would take a discovery of blockbuster impact—it was hard to conceive where it could come from—that would do more than change details in a study like mine already grounded on so various an accumulation of evidence. Since there was no explosion, the total effect was to my advantage. As Freeman began to fade, his volumes going out of print, this new uncompleted project frightened away any competition on a large scale.[26]

Vindication—if Flexner needed any—came in the early 1980s, when Hollywood producer David Gerber approached Flexner's lawyer about the possibility of producing a television miniseries based on his biography of Washington. Much had changed since 1951, when the movie *When the Redskins Rode* graced the big screen. Washington still had not hit the big time—probably his biggest role came in a 1972 episode of *Bewitched*, titled "George Washington Zapped Here," in which Esmeralda summoned him from the past by mistake and police arrested him for speaking in public without a permit—but Flexner's biography, as he proudly boasted, had "replaced the marble image with a warm and appealing human being," making him a more attractive leading man.[27] The political landscape was more welcoming, too. President Ronald Reagan took office in 1981 as a self-professed Washington admirer and frequently evoked the first president—

often in a religious context—in his speeches. Reagan's calls for a return to traditional American values dovetailed nicely with the 250th anniversary of Washington's birth in 1982 to spark a surge of renewed interest in the Founder. Flexner, no admirer of Reagan, stood foremost as a man who believed in Washington's greatness, and as the popular biographer who had brought him alive for a new generation of Americans.

General Motors, the major sponsor of the TV miniseries, expressed some concerns at first about associating with a project that might seek to humanize Washington by attempting to besmirch his reputation. Sally Fairfax especially worried the GM executives, for Flexner's almost obsessive interest in her as Washington's "dark love" was well known.[28] The producers consequently toned down aspects of their affair. Sally, ravishingly portrayed by former Charlie's Angel Jaclyn Smith, is omnipresent in the first installment of the miniseries, but although she and George flirt copiously and exchange yearning glances, they engage in nothing more intimate than a brief though passionate hug. No stranger to the art of compromise in pursuit of profit and popularity, Flexner enjoyed the celebrity treatment meted out to him during shooting, and wisely kept his mouth shut.

Once Sally disappears from the scene, however, the miniseries loses momentum. Barry Bostwick is a serviceable George, handsome and amiable if not charismatic, but generally predictable. Martha, portrayed by former teen star Patty Duke, appears tiny, dumpy, and insignificant by his side. Their courtship, in keeping with Flexner's own view, is formal and stiff, with Washington hiding an obvious contempt for his future mate beneath prepared phrases and forced smiles. Scenes of Washington's childhood and his home life with Martha's children seem borrowed straight out of the TV series *Little House on the Prairie*, with an appropriately cloying sound track. Society is clean, bright, and orderly, with blacks and natives relegated almost entirely to the periphery, and aside from Lloyd Bridges as laughably bewhiskered mountain man Caleb Quinn, who follows Washington everywhere through the French and Indian War, the characters are generally unremarkable despite the all-star cast. Although the first installment of the miniseries did well and was syndicated worldwide, ratings declined precipitously thereafter. Flexner ascribed this, probably with good reason, to the almost total absence of "sex and violence."

Though the miniseries did not achieve the smashing success for which Flexner and the producers had hoped, it certainly broke new ground. For the first time, Washington had starred in a quality Hollywood production and reentered the national spotlight. He seemed human again—free to tread the paths of myth and folklore, and to come alive in the popular imagination. Flexner deserved much of the credit for this piece of magic, even if the spell demanded the sacrifice of some truth. "The sun never sets on Flexner," his friends flattered him.[29] Of all his accomplishments, his greatest had been his last. He had served as George Washington's indispensable man.

CHAPTER 8

The Living Myth

I N THE AUTUMN OF 1944, Edith Ellis heard a voice. Seventy-two years old and nearly blind with severe glaucoma, she had made her living as a popular playwright from before World War I until the mid-1930s. She had also found another calling. As her stage writing career faded, she developed her aptitude as a spiritualist medium attuned to hearing voices from the other side. From her New York City apartment she conducted séances and consulted with fellow psychics on the intricacies of "etheric research," experimenting with various mechanical devices designed to make contact with the spirits of the dead. The devices failed, but Ellis found other methods of crossing over. The spirit of Wilfred Brandon, who had been killed during the Revolutionary War at the tender age of nineteen, particularly troubled her, and through a long series of grueling trances he transmitted his life story to her. Ellis published

Brandon's revelations in *Open the Door!* (1935), *Incarnation: A Plea from the Masters* (1936), and *We Knew These Men* (1942), all with the prestigious New York publishing house of Alfred A. Knopf. In 1944, however, Brandon seemed to become preoccupied with ethereal matters and less inclined to chat with material beings. Ellis's mystical ears thereupon attuned themselves to a new voice that spoke with greater confidence and authority: that of George Washington.[1]

Ellis spent 110 days conversing with Washington. He had much to say. In particular, he wished to reveal "the content of his heart and soul," his very "emotional being," so that Americans should learn to reach beyond the "frozen figure" that historians had constructed in his place.[2] Ellis listened attentively to the hollow whisperings of his fourth-dimensional voice and scratched out reams of hasty notes that her young secretary, Harriet von Tobel, transcribed into a prose manuscript. Ellis lived in the age of debunking, however, and from either fear of mockery or lack of energy she never got around to preparing the manuscript for publication. She died in 1961, and her secretary placed the manuscript in storage, where it remained for two more decades.

In 1983, Harriet von Tobel dusted off Ellis's manuscript and submitted it to a small publishing house, Stillpoint. Stillpoint, at that time something of a fly-by-night affair, somehow lost track of the manuscript, and von Tobel returned to obscurity. Meanwhile, one of Stillpoint's three founders, Caroline Myss, rose above her humble beginnings and became famous. A former journalist, she developed an interest in mysticism and holistic health, and in the 1980s she devoted herself to becoming a self-described "medical intuitive." Miraculously, she could determine a patient's complete physical, psychological, and family history without knowing anything more than his or her age and name. Her two books on medical intuition and holistic healing, *Anatomy of the Spirit: The Seven Stages of Power and Healing* (1996) and *Why People Don't Heal and How They Can* (1997), became *New York Times* bestsellers, flying off bookstore shelves by the millions in eighteen different languages.

Then came 9/11. Myss, who had taken to studying America's mystical history—a subject beloved of mystical and occult writers since the early twentieth century—recalled the Washington autobiography she had misplaced almost two decades earlier, and began to think of its application to the troubles of the present age. It remained in her thoughts over the next few years as she catapulted even further toward international stardom. Her book *Sacred Contracts: Awakening Your Divine Potential* (2003), which applied her research in mystical history to the principles of everyday living, vaulted her again onto the *New York Times* bestseller list, as did another book, *Invisible Acts of Power*, published in 2004. Oprah Winfrey sealed Myss's rise to glory by inviting her on to her show and enshrining her mystical principles on the official Oprah website. Myss founded the Caroline Myss Educational Institute, and people flocked to her speeches and workshops on intuitive healing.[3]

Washington's moment had arrived. Renewing contact with von Tobel, Myss reacquired the rights to the Ellis manuscript and brought it to publication in 2005. *An Autobiography of George Washington*, introduced by Myss with an essay on America's "sacred contract," did not reach the national bestseller lists, but (thanks in no small part to her fame) it outsold many standard Washington biographies. "Washington's autobiography," Myss told her readers, "is part of the mystical literature meant to be unveiled to America at this time—a piece of a grand cosmic plan."[4]

Washington's spirit corrected numerous popular misconceptions about his personality and life as he revealed the grand cosmic plan. To begin with, he had been born in 1724, not 1732, and his real birthday should properly be celebrated on November 14. "All records that I know of," he whispered to Ellis, "have been based on the British accounts, which were never really authentic." The cherry tree incident was false—Washington resented the "dreadful blight" that Parson Weems had placed upon his character, and no doubt vindictively hunted his spirit through the ether—but he had enjoyed a colorful childhood. He spent those days romping through the woods, hunting squirrels and other game with his father, a "famous sportsman," roasting popcorn over the fire, and joking with his housekeeper slave, "Mammy Banty."

Young Washington didn't like his studies, especially history, and his scholarly, older brother Lawrence cruelly cuffed him for being slow at his lessons. Frequently George would escape his schoolbooks to run off with a local villager named Lightfoot, who told him exciting stories of famous military heroes. George especially liked to hear about the legendary Duke of Wellington and how he had progressed from an awkward lad to a great general, famously besting Napoleon at the Battle of Waterloo in 1815. "I was inspired by this romantic figure," the spirit recalled, "and decided that I, too, could make a career as a soldier."[5]

As a teenager, Washington signed up for the "Virginia Volunteers," causing his mother to faint and his father to stammer in rage, and he went off for a time to fight Indians in Maryland as an enlisted soldier serving under a Colonel Corliss.

Returning home, George reconnected with his father, Augustine, and learned about business and politics. The history books said that Augustine had died when George was eleven years old, but no matter. Augustine was an important politician in the colony and got into trouble by speaking out violently in the House of Burgesses against British rule, causing him to be dubbed "a firebrand, a rebel."

George followed his father's political career closely but still found time for personal pleasures. He had several mistresses, including a quadroon, and had a passionate but brief affair with Sally Fairfax. One day George teased Sally about her habit of pouting when she was with him. "You ugly brute, I hate you!" she cried, and ran off to shack up with a member of his regiment, by whom she had nine children. George then traveled to Cuba, where he caught smallpox—producing such hideous scarring that he was ever thereafter shy around women—and returned to fight a terrible battle at Quebec, where he was defeated and humiliated. He then left to fight the French and Indian War, causing his father to burst into tears. After a number of battles—including a terrible affair under General Edward Braddock at Fort Pitt, where Washington was one of only eight survivors—he served garrison duty in Williamsburg, Virginia, under a General Forsyth. Unfortunately, Washington got caught up in horse racing and broke his collarbone in an accident. A short time later, he was kicked out of the service for dueling.[6]

Washington's troubles continued. He got into the habit of going to the barn twice a day to swig hard cider from a jug, and struggled with alcoholism as a result. Though a devout Christian—he studied scriptures and said his prayers every night—Washington was tormented by psychic visions. One

day he had the disconcerting experience of meeting and falling into conversation with his own disembodied astral body.
His mother died shortly afterward and his father weakened,
but instead of staying at home to tend his family's farm, poor
George had to go off and join the New York militia around
Boston. He was serving there as a colonel during the Battle
of Bunker Hill, and after hearing that war had broken out, he
resigned from British service in order to support his country's
cause. For a time he acted as a brigadier general, but Congress
eventually promoted him to commander in chief.

Washington led his army to victory at Trenton in 1779
and then marched off to spend the winter of 1779–80 at Valley
Forge. He went into that terrible encampment with 600 men,
but only 132 came out alive. George and Martha, whom by
the way he had married, huddled there in rags, gobbling in-
sects, gnawing tree bark, and nibbling on rat carcasses. At
one point he fainted when he tried to stick a shovel into the
ground. Luckily, Aaron Burr kept him and his soldiers alive
by sending in, from time to time, braces of rabbits and sacks
of wheat. Thenceforward, whenever Washington mentioned
his name, his soldiers would murmur "God bless Aaron Burr."
Spiritual and psychic experiences also kept Washington going,
and for clarity—the spirit was prone to become a little vague
at times—Myss helpfully inserted a full-length account of the
wondrous Valley Forge vision.[7]

Leaving Valley Forge in March 1780, Washington immediately zoomed off to Yorktown, joined up with Lafayette,
and captured the British forces arrayed there under the command of General William Howe. Washington remained weak
from his winter ordeal, and when he reached out to shake
hands with General Howe after signing their "peace pact,"

he fainted and collapsed in a heap at his erstwhile opponent's feet. "This poor chap has never won a victory before," Howe glibly remarked. "It is too much for him." He then turned to Lafayette and chatted with him for a couple of hours while Washington snored in the mud. At this point in the story the Washington spirit apparently grew bored, and he passed quickly over his career as president before briefly recounting his death of a heart attack in the autumn of 1798.[8]

The Washington spirit, Myss admitted, became a little "foggy" on the facts from time to time. He admitted as much himself, but explained away the discrepancies between his narration and the established historical record by claiming that all the true documents of his life had been either destroyed or deliberately falsified.[9] Myss more charitably suggested that the spirit's words had probably just become a little garbled during transmission through the ether. No medium was perfect, after all, and poor Caroline Ellis had been well past her prime in 1944. The spirit-phone on which she had been working at the time had failed to function properly, and so she had had to rely upon her own declining faculties. No wonder that she missed a word here and there, or mistook "Barbados" for "Cuba."

THE FACT THAT a popular author could publish and endorse the Ellis-Washington spirit transcript in the first decade of the twenty-first century, with nary a critic in sight, provides an indication of how far Washington has outdistanced the debunkers. The floodgates have opened, and mythmaking has taken on new energy. The quarter century that has passed since the premiere of the *George Washington* miniseries in 1984 has witnessed an explosion of Founder folklore not seen since the nineteenth century. Some of these modern myths amount to little more than tabloid history, equally trivial and absurd. Others permeate journalism and literature, both popular and academic. In the aggregate, they reflect a profound change in Americans' attitude toward their history. Once again, as in the era of Parson Weems, accuracy has taken a distinct backseat to imaginative storytelling.

Nowhere is this trend more apparent than in the modern mythology pertaining to West Ford, Washington's infamous "slave child." Linda Allen Bryant, a West Ford descendant, popularized this story in the late 1990s in the wake of the revelation that Thomas Jefferson had most likely fathered at least one child by his slave Sally Hemings. According to Bryant, George Washington consorted with a slave girl named Venus, who belonged to his brother John Augustine Washington, and with her fathered a child, West Ford. John Augustine lived at Bushfield plantation, about 95 miles from Mount Vernon, and George visited there only rarely, but Bryant claims that he did so often enough to form an extended relationship. Venus did, in fact, have a mulatto son named West Ford, who was set free by the will of John Augustine Washington's wife, Hannah Bushrod Washington. Ford moved to Mount Vernon in 1802 and was a well-known figure in Alexandria until his death in the mid-nineteenth century.[10]

Bryant's revelation about George Washington's secret past, which became public in 1996, attracted tremendous media interest. She appeared on television as the guest of honor on *Today*, *Frontline*, the History Channel, and MSNBC, and was interviewed and described approvingly by *Newsweek*, the *New York Times*, the *Washington Post*, and other magazines and newspapers. In 2000, PBS produced a documentary, *George and Venus*, highlighting the Ford family's attempt to secure official recognition of their claim by the Mount Vernon Ladies' Association. Bryant capped off her campaign in 2001 by publishing a book titled *I Cannot Tell a Lie: The True Story of George Washington's African American Descendants*. Pulling no punches, she boldly called Washington "one of my great grandfathers" and West Ford "his son."[11]

I Cannot Tell a Lie overflows with gripping scenes. On George's first visit to Bushfield, his brother John Augustine encounters Venus on a staircase and pulls her aside. "Venus," he says with a nervous catch in his throat, "you get yourself to Master George's room. He . . . ah . . . needs comforting and has asked for you." She obeys, having no choice in the matter, and becomes George's regular mistress, following him to Mount Vernon. "Only he," writes Bryant, "could touch her sexually," although he apparently never knew that she served him against her will.[12] When Venus gives birth to West Ford at Bushfield in 1785, her mother, Jenny, looks on in astonishment:

> "Lawsy, that sure be the whitest slave baby I ever done seen," remarked Jenny as she took the child from her daughter. "Them Washingtons ain't gonna like this one bit, but don't you worry, little one, you gots me and your mammy to love you," she cooed to the baby. Her voice took on a wistful note. "I sure do wish your pappy could 'of seen this here chile."[13]

Washington reacts coldly to the infant during a poignant encounter at Valley Forge and subsequently severs his relationship with the unhappy girl.

Bryant presents her tale as "narrative history," but without presenting a scrap of documentation. The evidence for her assertion that Washington fathered West Ford by Venus amounts to nothing more than a few letters suggesting that he did on occasion visit Bushfield, although whether he ever actually did so is disputable. Beyond that, she relies solely on unsourced "personal anecdotes" and family traditions in which she changes names and other details in order to protect privacy. "Venus," she asserts, "revealed the identity of the father to the son, who in turn told his son. Thus, the Ford family's origins were preserved in an oral document that has endured for over two centuries."[14] On the same basis, one might as well assume that half the population of the United States is descended from Pocahontas. Moreover, Bryant cannot cite a single instance before the 1980s of a member of West Ford's family, let alone an outsider, claiming that Washington had been his father. Searching for some form of contemporary evidence—which exists, be it noted, for the claim that Jefferson fathered a child by Sally Hemings—Bryant can only fall back on the old slanders that Washington slept with Sweet Kate, the washerwoman's daughter, and that he died as a result of a heart attack brought on by an assignation with an overseer's wife. She also cites rumors that some former employees of Mount Vernon had seen, back in the 1940s, a diary in which Washington kept a record of his various mistresses.

The Venus slave child story is an apparent attempt to piggyback on the Sally Hemings scandal and might ordinarily not merit serious consideration. Publicity can work wonders, however, and the story has entered popular discourse as ineffably as Weems's cherry tree—with the difference that Venus is fresher, more relevant to contemporary concerns about race, and therefore more exciting. In an art exhibit at the Volta gallery in New York City in 2009, British pop artist Annie Kevans immortalized Venus by including her, along with Sally Fairfax, in a series of paintings titled "All the Presidents' Girls." "The portraits may or may not be based on real documentation," Kevans admitted before tagging on the postmodernist mantra, "Can we ever know the truth?"[15]

SPURIOUS WASHINGTON QUOTATIONS, disseminated in the name of politics and religion, have also gained renewed popularity at the beginning of the twenty-first century. For example, gun rights advocates often quote Washington as saying to the second session of the first U.S. Congress:

> Firearms stand next in importance to the Constitution itself. They are the American people's liberty, teeth and keystone under independence. The church, the plow, the prairie wagon and citizens' firearms are indelibly related. From the hour the pilgrims landed to the present day, events, occurrences and tendencies prove that, to ensure peace, security and happiness, the rifle and pistol are equally indispensable. Every corner of this land knows firearms, and more than 99 and 99/100 percent of them by their silence indicate that they are in safe and sane hands. The very atmosphere of firearms anywhere and everywhere restrains evil influence. They deserve a place of honor with all that's good. When firearms go, all goes. We need them every hour.[16]

Even the obviously anachronistic reference to the "prairie wagon" isn't enough to keep people from using this spurious quotation, which is entirely fictitious.

During the presidential election campaign of 2008, Senator John McCain spoke of carrying a paper in his pocket bearing a quotation he attributed to George Washington. "The willingness with which our young people are likely to serve in any war, no matter how justified," the quotation read, "shall be directly proportional as to how they perceive the veterans of earlier wars were treated and appreciated by their nation." The *National Review Online*, after contacting the Papers of George Washington, called McCain out on this spurious quotation, but politicians and activists, both Republican and Democratic, continue to cite it in support of veterans' rights.

The so-called Washington prayer, modified from Washington's circular letter to the states of June 8, 1783, in order to indicate that he was a practicing Christian, is also quoted frequently in the corridors of power. Speaking in the House of Representatives on April 21, 2009, Congresswoman Michele Bachmann quoted the spurious prayer, and concluded: "Mr. Speaker, our first President, George Washington, insisted on his inauguration day as the first President of this great country, that unless the citizens of our country imitate the example of Jesus Christ, that we would not be a happy Nation. What a clear contrast between our first President and our current President."

Speaking to the Democratic National Convention on August 28, 2008, Democrat Al Gore referred to "the American principle first laid down by General George Washington, when he prohibited the torture of captives because it would

bring, in his words, 'shame, disgrace and ruin' to our nation."
The quotation was correct—it came from Washington's letter
to Benedict Arnold of September 17, 1775—but actually had
nothing to do with torture. Instead, Washington was encour-
aging religious toleration and emphasizing the importance of
treating Canadian Catholics with dignity and respect. But at
least Gore had his larger point correct, even if the evidence
he used to justify it was misleading—Washington did work
throughout the war to ensure the humane treatment of prisoners on both sides.

Since the late twentieth century, advocates of the legal-
ization of marijuana have spread stories that Washington
grew the hallucinogen as a crop and even smoked it. Washington did grow hemp, which produces no narcotic effects,
but he cultivated it only briefly, and solely for industrial purposes: the production of paper, cloth, rope, oakum, and fuel.
Most Virginia colonists grew hemp, in fact, for the simple
reason that the House of Burgesses promoted its growth—
again, for industrial purposes—with a generous bounty. In
Washington's case, he experimented with growing hemp
between 1765 and 1767 and again with a different variety
in the 1790s, but he found the crop unprofitable and discon-
tinued it. Partisan websites and tracts nevertheless overflow
with confident assertions that hemp was a "primary crop"
at Mount Vernon and that Washington smoked, dealt, and
grew marijuana.[17] A spurious quote, "make the most of the
Indian hemp seed and sow it everywhere," has also gained
widespread currency.[18] Many of the same people who assert
that Washington smoked pot also claim that he got along
well with Lafayette and Alexander Hamilton because he was
a closet homosexual.

* * *

WASHINGTON HAS ALSO AT TIMES settled even deeper within the realm of the bizarre. In 1998 a remarkable story floated around the Internet and eventually into the email inboxes of staff at the Papers of George Washington project at the University of Virginia. One Quentin Burde of Edinburgh, an "independent Scots historian" specializing in extraterrestrial phenomena, claimed to have discovered several volumes of Washington's Revolutionary War diaries moldering in a Scottish archive. The diary made reference to several meetings between the commander in chief and a group of beings he referred to as "Greenskins," who lived in a luminescent globe in the snow-choked woods behind Valley Forge. "Until now," said Burde, "historians have assumed Washington was referring to a tribe that used green war paint," while the commander in chief himself "probably thought he was talking with an extremely talented Indian war chief, or a medicine man with powers bordering on the magical." Upon careful study, however, Burde determined that the globe's tendency to vanish and reappear rapidly and the Greenskins' willingness to supply Washington with advice, information on enemy movements, and "superior technology" proved that these were indeed creatures from another planet.[19]

Washington's reincarnation, alive and well and living in Cincinnati, contacted the Washington Papers project in the early 1970s, and modestly offered his assistance in making sense of his illustrious former life. On this subject, there is obviously room for reasoned scholarly debate, for it seems that Washington has reincarnated simultaneously into several different people. Walter Semkiw, M.D., founder of the

Institute for the Integration of Science, Intuition, and Spirit and a popular advocate of past-life regression, has determined, with the help of the Egyptian spirit guide Ahtun Re, that the present-day reincarnation of Washington is none other than General Tommy Franks, although Franks apparently remains unaware of his true identity. Martha has also reincarnated as Franks's wife, Cathy.[20]

Washington's ghost, meanwhile, wanders the country even as his soul simultaneously inhabits the bodies of several living people. As a matter of fact, he's been flitting around since the nineteenth century, with intervals of dormancy in skeptical times. In the 1870s, spiritualist mediums thrilled audiences by materializing Washington during their séances, although the results did not always live up to expectations. In Maine, reported an 1877 article in the *New York Times*, a medium foolishly conjured up a Washington clad in patent leather boots and a Piccadilly collar. Another medium inadvertently snatched out of the spirit world "an undersized Washington, not over four feet eight inches in height, and was hissed because Washington's back hair accidentally came down, accompanied by a shower of hair-pins." Yet another medium, performing onstage in Oshkosh, conjured up a tall, properly attired Washington clutching a Farewell Address in his hand. Unfortunately, the spirit slipped on an orange peel that had been tossed onstage by a skeptic, and pandemonium ensued.

When the stately ghost sat violently down, his sword and his Farewell Address flying in different directions, the spectators were pained, but their suspicions would not have been aroused had not Washington immediately remarked, "By gosh!" This unguarded expression, together with the fact that the Farewell Address was captured by an irreverent person, and found to be nothing but a certificate of stock in a petroleum company, aroused a great deal of indignation, which . . . took the form of prehistoric eggs and the limp bodies of specially prepared cats, and ultimately led to the abrupt departure of the medium from the town.[21]

Washington's ghost dwelt more inconspicuously in shadowy corners and dark stairwells, frightening visitors to Mount Vernon by stalking through the halls "with martial tread and clank of astral sword in spectral scabbard," and terrifying servants by taking up residence in one of his favorite old clocks. The undead general also tormented secessionist Senator John C. Calhoun, haunting his dreams and burning into his hand a dark blotch—the traitor's mark by which Benedict Arnold had become known in the next world.[22] Recent versions of this tale have the ghost appearing to Calhoun not in a dream but in waking life and impolitely flinging a skeleton into his arms. The bones, claimed the specter, were the remains of an American Revolutionary War soldier who had been hung by the British. "He gave," moaned the ghost as Calhoun cowered in terror, "his life to establish the Union."[23]

Washington's ghost went dormant for a time in the first half of the twentieth century, or only presented himself to true believers who could keep their mouths shut. Debunkers evidently frightened him. During the last quarter of the century, however, the antiquated specter perked up, and by the time the twenty-first century dawned he proudly rattled his chains from coast to coast. Washington's ghost has been seen in Annapolis, Valley Forge, Philadelphia, Williamsburg, and of course Alexandria, where he is a staple of spirit tours. He rides his white horse about historic Woodlawn Plantation near Alexandria—a veritable den of spectral activity of all kinds—and a former employee of Mount Vernon witnessed his transparent figure sitting at his desk and writing with a quill pen. When the ghost saw the employee standing in the doorway, he beckoned her to come in, but then rudely vanished as soon as she entered the room.[24] Washington has also floated across the Atlantic Ocean in order to haunt his family's ancestral home at Sunderland in the United Kingdom.

The most popular current Washington ghost story was dramatized in a 2008 episode of *Haunted Travels* on TV's Travel Channel. On July 2, 1863, the focal point of the Civil War Battle of Gettysburg shifted to Little Round Top on the Union left flank, where Confederate troops attempted to dislodge Colonel Joshua Lawrence Chamberlain's 20th Maine Regiment. Fighting raged back and forth for hours, until the Federals ran entirely out of ammunition. With another Confederate attack imminent, Chamberlain pondered his next move. The decision, however, was taken out of his hands. As the bluecoats waited, the figure of an officer mounted on a shining white stallion appeared before them, dressed in Revolutionary War uniform and brandishing a flaming sword. It rode up and down the line, mysteriously boosting Union morale as it passed. "Fix bayonets! Charge!" it finally cried, and led Chamberlain's men downhill in a furious charge against the Rebels, who fired at the figure but without scoring a hit. The charge routed the Confederates, turning the tide of the entire battle, but as it ended the figure disappeared.

Only later did Chamberlain and his men connect the dots and realize that they had followed the ghost of George Washington. Some said the secretary of war, Edwin M. Stanton, ordered an official inquiry into the affair, and gathered piles of eyewitness testimony that the government subsequently suppressed.[25]

This story originated with Chamberlain himself, but it has changed considerably since its first telling. In June 1913, *Hearst's Magazine* published an article by Chamberlain titled "Through Blood and Fire at Gettysburg."[26] During the Union army's march to Gettysburg—not at Little Round Top—all sorts of rumors swept through the ranks as the troops contemplated the impending battle. Some said that the recently dismissed General George McClellan, much loved by the men, had retaken command of the army. Others claimed to have witnessed various mystical phenomena. "Now from a dark angle of the roadside," Chamberlain wrote, "came a whisper, whether from earthly or unearthly voice one cannot feel quite sure, that the august form of Washington had been seen that afternoon at sunset riding over the Gettysburg hills. Let no one smile at me! I half believed it myself,—so did the powers of the other world draw nigh!"

One month after the publication of this article, according to a newspaper account, a reporter asked Chamberlain to elaborate on the Washington ghost story.[27] He considered the question in silence for a while before answering. "Yes," he finally admitted, "that report was circulated through our lines and I have no doubt that it had a tremendous psychological effect in inspiring the men. Doubtless it was a superstition, but yet who among us can say that such a thing was impossible? . . . I do believe that we were enveloped by the powers of the other world that day and who shall say that Washington was not among the number of those who aided the country that he founded?"[28] There the matter remained for decades. In the late twentieth century, popular ghost story writers dug up the tired old tale and gave it a new twist by transferring the action to Little Round Top and adding details of Washington's figure riding up and down the lines and ordering the charge.

WASHINGTON'S GHOST has also become a media celebrity. In 2008, he made an appearance in the conservative satirical movie *An American Carol*, in which Jon Voight, playing a decidedly Christian Founding ghost, castigated a character named Michael Malone (a stand-in for liberal filmmaker Michael Moore) for his lack of patriotism by showing him the carnage at the World Trade Center after 9/11. In material form, however, Washington has yet to hit the big screen, aside from two minor roles in *Revolution* (1985) and *The Patriot* (2000). On television, he has enjoyed much greater success. Jeff Daniels played Washington in *The Crossing* (2000), and Kelsey Grammer depicted him in *Benedict Arnold: A Question of Honor* (2003). Washington has also appeared in the miniseries *John Adams* (2008), and he played a dubious role as a child-eating cannibal in 2007 in an episode of the Showtime series *Masters of Horror* titled "The Washingtonians."

Historical facts of all sorts are routinely distorted or ignored in these productions. *The Crossing*, for example, repeats many old, long-discredited myths—such as the story of drunken Hessians at the Battle of Trenton—while Jeff Daniels channels a hot-tempered, foulmouthed Washington straight out of Rupert Hughes. "Move your fat ass, Henry," he snorts at the rotund Colonel Henry Knox as they step into a boat. "Don't swing your balls or you'll swamp the boat." Soldiers, meanwhile, guffaw nearby. Kelsey Grammer portrays an equally vulgar Founder in *Benedict Arnold*, reacting to news of his general's treason by publicly howling, "Let's hang the son of a bitch!" Such ridiculously implausible characterizations convey the continuing uncertainty with which Hollywood views Washington. Though far removed from the wooden symbolism of the 1950s, he has yet to settle in as a Hollywood leading man.

Even documentary filmmakers struggle to present an approachable Washington. In the quest for exciting stories, they frequently miscast certain episodes in his life, such as the romance with Sally Fairfax, or inadvertently present fabricated renditions of his experiences. A 2008 National Geographic Channel documentary titled *The Real George Washington*, for example, uncritically retells the spurious story of spy John Honeyman at the Battle of Trenton. Small budgets lay behind some of the blunders. The producers of *Washington the Warrior*, a History Channel documentary broadcast in 2006, worked hard and largely successfully to present an exciting but factual account of Washington's military career, but budgetary constraints forced them to economize by filming military and civilian reenactments in Lithuania, and with largely Lithuanian casts. Many of the resulting mistakes in this and other documentaries—Indians throwing tomahawks, anachronistic uniforms, and the like—may bother only professional nitpickers, but Washington also sometimes appears in a distorted light.

Abundant resources of money and good intentions are not infallible antidotes to distortion. In the early 2000s, several documentary and big-screen filmmakers vied for a contract to produce a centerpiece multimillion-dollar movie for Mount Vernon's massive state-of-the-art visitor center, scheduled to open in 2006. Their proposals ranged from pedantically dull to hopelessly disjointed, and after numerous false starts Mount Vernon's administrators began to despair of finishing the movie in time for the visitor center's grand opening. California-based Greystone Communications, an Emmy-winning producer of television documentaries such as *Ancient Prophecies and Angels, Haunted History, Civil War Combat,* and *The Big House: Prisons in America,* came to the rescue with a slam-bang proposal for a movie that would focus on some of the most exciting moments of Washington's military career. Based on a script by Oscar-nominated screenwriter Lionel Chetwynd and backed by an experienced director and crew, the proposed film seemed perfectly suited to inspire visitors—especially young ones—with an appreciation for Washington's dramatic life.

Just a few problems had to be sorted out. Concerned that the film should reflect their commitment to accuracy, Mount Vernon asked a team of historians—including myself—to review Chetwynd's script. We discovered several errors and misconceptions, including scenes of a heroic young Washington hauling a gibbering, half-frozen Christopher Gist from the Allegheny River in 1754 (the opposite actually took place); Washington backslapping and chatting amiably with militia privates around a campfire during the Revolutionary War; and Washington preparing to cross the Delaware River on Christmas Day, 1776—from an encampment located at Valley Forge.

At this late stage, Mount Vernon did not have the luxury of starting again from scratch. Besides, Chetwynd and Grey-

stone's producers amiably agreed to amend the script according to our directions and promised to adhere scrupulously
to fact in every stage of production. This would be no run-
of-the-mill Hollywood movie, they said, but a testament to
Washington's greatness. Putting the seal to this commitment,
they offered to hire me—a professional historian—as an on-set
consultant, and promised to defer to my wisdom in all things.
I agreed, and we sealed the deal over dinner in the director's
house at Mount Vernon. Over cocktails, the producers pulled
me aside and chided me gently to remember that good moviemaking required the freedom to exercise dramatic license.
Addled by alcohol, I nodded agreeably. If my mind had been
clearer, I might have anticipated what I had let myself in for,
and fled for the hills.

Cast and crew assembled near Harpers Ferry early in
2006 to film Washington's troops crossing the Delaware.
The bitter cold and wind abetted the work of the artificial
snow machines, but it also tested the dedication of the dozens
of reenactors who had assembled in the guise of bedraggled
Continental soldiers. They came in all shapes and sizes—old
and young, white and black, portly, muscular, and emaciated. Some were cranky and unapproachable, others childish
and hyperactive—in short, just everyday folks who in real life
were students, bankers, lawyers, grocery store clerks, retirees,
former Special Forces officers, and the like. Without exception, though, they knew more about eighteenth-century life
and warfare than the vast majority of academics—certainly
more than I did. They worked for a pittance, but without
complaint. Nor did they jockey for position in front of the
camera. They had come strictly for the joy of plying their
hobby and sharing their knowledge.

Greystone's crew and production staff did not—outwardly at least—share my esteem for the reenactors. Instead, to my surprise, the two groups regarded each other suspiciously and at times with outright animosity. The reenactors, as is their eternal wont, were prone to nitpick. A button out of place, a cap badge awry, a medal from the wrong era, and especially— God forbid—the wrong type of weapon instantly provoked cries of "Fubar," meaning "f——d up beyond all recognition." The antics of these latter-day "Stitch Nazis"—as they have been uncharitably, but not inaccurately called—infuriated the movie people, who insisted that they would accept correction only from the officially designated expert source: me.

While flattering, the producers' professed faith in my good judgment was not always justified. Like many academics, I knew a lot about big-picture subjects, but when it got down to specifics I was as ignorant as any preschooler. I provided some useful advice on Washington's opinions on discipline and military etiquette, and on one occasion I intervened to prevent the movie folks from casting a group of elderly, unshaven, and sunken-cheeked gentlemen as Washington's personal bodyguard. On the finer points of drill, uniforms, and weaponry, however, I preferred to defer to the reenactors. But since they were typically not on speaking terms with the movie crew, I soon found myself acting more as a courier than a historical advisor, jogging over to consult the reenactors about hats, muskets, or coat buttons and then jogging back to pass the information on to the director and crew. By the end of the shoot, as Washington stood proudly in the prow of a boat crewed by reenactors, who rowed him sullenly across a frozen field (the Delaware River would be added later via computer graphics in the studio), I had begun to feel somewhat adrift.

The crew reassembled at Mount Vernon in the summer of 2006 for the central shoot. For the first few days, all seemed cozy and amiable. The actors portraying George and Martha Washington—Sebastian Roché and Caroline Goodall— accepted criticism with professionalism and good grace, collaborating with myself and Mount Vernon's expert staff to render intimate family scenes with both emotional power and accuracy. Elsewhere, a different tone prevailed. Off near Washington's restored eight-sided barn, hundreds of reenactors and film crew assembled to film the primary battle scenes, which would re-create General Edward Braddock's defeat on the Monongahela River in 1755. At first glance, all seemed united in industriousness and a sense of purpose. Closer inspection revealed such tension and hostility between the reenactors and the movie producers and crew that I feared something would blow.

Camped off on the edge of the estate in jumbled tents, the reenactors welcomed me and my young son—whom I had brought along to witness moviemaking in action—with open arms, and proudly showed off their uniforms and accoutrements. Yet beneath the apparent joviality they were becoming increasingly enraged with a film that they had come to regard as a historical atrocity. One morning, one of them waylaid me on the way to the set with a stark warning. "Mr. Historian," he said, "this movie is going to have your name on it. And you're going to look like a fool." He seemed to expect me to snort with disdain and walk by. Instead, I stopped to talk with him—an entirely new experience on this film set, judging by the startled look on his face. Detecting a willing ear, a group of his comrades gathered around and unloaded their pent-up frustrations on me.

That night, a large group of reenactors sat in their tents and filled a yellow notepad with a list of twenty-three points on which the moviemakers had gone wrong. Most had to do with how soldiers dressed, formed, and fought and how officers gave orders under fire. Also, Indians did not throw tomahawks or hurl spears, and "warriors did not swing down from tree limbs here or anywhere." But many of their complaints had to do with Washington. He could not, they said, have reloaded his pistol under fire. He never would have presumed to tell British general Braddock what he should do. And "it would be nearly impossible," the reenactors insisted in criticism of one of the centerpiece action scenes, "for Washington to knock away a line of muskets at fixed bayonets without spearing his horse or himself." They solemnly submitted the list to me the next morning, and I duly noted it as their manifesto.

The movie folks were unhappy, too. They regarded the reenactors as pests who complained about everything while messing up innumerable shots. In one episode that I witnessed, a line of redcoats fired a volley at a ragged group of reenactors dressed as French Canadians. According to script, the latter fired their muskets and then turned and ran. As the camera rolled, however, one of the reenactors stopped running and turned back to retrieve his shoe, which he had lost in the mud. The comical element in this was lost on the film crew, who cursed and fumed; film was expensive, and they had to keep to a tight schedule. The stunt director, a longtime professional, abused the reenactors with his every breath— and since he was an ex-Marine, his language was ceaselessly colorful. The worst of their sins, in his book, was their inability to die properly. Shot or tomahawked, they gently lay down in the grass as if going to sleep. Disgustedly he ejected them from the central battle scenes and used his own boys instead—professional stuntmen who had worked on *Saving Private Ryan* and other big-time action movies.

For me, the filming of the battle scenes degenerated into hair-tearing chaos as I rushed to and fro in an attempt to correct errors and soothe ruffled egos on both sides. At times I expected the reenactors to break ranks and storm the little fortress around the director and his cameras, or to pull Washington off his horse. Meanwhile, Indians rushed pell-mell through the woods, dropped out of trees, and charged fixed lines of redcoats, throwing their tomahawks about with gusto. I stopped one of them to ask what he would fight with now that his only weapon had embedded itself in a redcoat's chest ten yards away. Bemusedly he pointed to a tiny ceremonial dagger hanging around his neck, then moved on. Elsewhere, an Indian busily tomahawked a soldier while another redcoat stood two feet away, calmly loading his musket. And into the fray rode Washington, waving his sword, rallying troops—and wearing a French cockade in his hat (filming stopped while it was replaced). Beside him rode his trusted confidant, Colonel Adam Stephen, sporting a Prince Valiant haircut. The woods around them were littered with comfortably reclining reenactors playing dead, discarded rubber muskets with crooked bayonets, and candy wrappers from the omnipresent traveling snack bar.

The climactic battle scene presented Washington at the center of a group of soldiers, all of whom were scripted to be shot and killed while he miraculously emerged unscathed. The producers boasted that this would constitute their "*Miami Vice* on the Monongahela," filmed in slow motion from an orbiting camera and later enhanced in the studio with battle sounds, music, and charming spurts of blood. Naturally, mere reenactors could have no place in this scene, so the stunt director gathered his own boys together, coached them carefully, and pumped them up like football players. The cameras rolled, and they went to work. Simulating the effects of getting hit by musket balls at a range of fifty to seventy-five yards—which normally would cause a man to snap sharply backward or topple over like a sack of meal—the stuntmen screamed hysterically, popped several feet into the air, performed backflips worthy of Olympic gymnasts, and hurled their muskets into the treetops. After shooting finished, they gathered round to watch their work on camera, and declared their approval with hoots and high fives. Meanwhile, a group of longtime reenactors rolled around in the leaves on a nearby hillock, laughing hysterically. I began to wonder whether the time had come to intervene.

Naively I approached the producer and suggested that the stuntmen might want to tone down their gymnastics and give the scene a degree of realism appropriate to eighteenth-century battle. At first he barred me from speaking to the director. Then, as I persisted—respectfully, and in a measured tone of voice—the producer burst into a screaming tirade, replete with curses, as my young son stood nearby. I was an idiot (and worse), a meddler, a busybody, a stuffy academic; I understood nothing about filmmaking or entertaining an audience. Appalled, I called in some Mount Vernon officials to calm him down and review the scene just filmed. Their arrival at first sent the producer only into further hysterics, but eventually he calmed down. Later, he, the film director, and the Mount Vernon officials responsible for overseeing the filming apologized for the outburst and promised me that the stuntmen's worst excesses would be toned down in the editing room. But the scene would stand as filmed. As I left the set with my son that afternoon, I met several reenactors. Their anger had turned to dejection. They didn't protest anymore, but muttered under their breath and shuffled slump-backed off to battle like the proverbial lambs to the slaughter. I did not return, and later asked for my name to be removed from the credits. It was not removed—but it *was* misspelled.

Greystone's final product, titled *We Fight to Be Free* and running twenty-four minutes, entertains millions of tourists as they pass through the orientation center on their way to George Washington's famous estate at Mount Vernon. By almost any standards, it is an unqualified success. Introduced by TV game show host Pat Sajak, it impresses visitors with a sense of Washington's bravery and humanity, and builds their enthusiasm for the coming tour. With the high-tech exhibits in the new visitor center, it helps to create a sense of intimacy with the great man that no dusty collection of curios in glass cases ever could have conveyed. Whether this could have been achieved without sacrificing realism—discarding, for example, Indians throwing tomahawks, soldiers doing backflips, and so on—is another question. It's worth asking, perhaps, whether moviemakers have ever tested their a priori assumption that the realistic is inevitably boring. In the meantime we're left with George Washington channeling Sonny Crockett of *Miami Vice* on the Monongahela.

George Washington stands at the crux of the conflict between academia and pop culture, between accuracy and entertainment. Rightly or wrongly, many Americans have developed the perception that facts are dull. Hollywood did not invent this idea. Almost from the moment Washington died—and indeed, while he was still alive—storytellers have knowingly embellished aspects of his life, sometimes deceptively and for profit, but more often simply to make him accessible to a wider audience. Academics have always railed against this trend. But if the debunkers of the 1920s and 1930s proved anything, they proved that stripping the gilded statue robs it of much of its public appeal. In their willingness to move beyond verifiable facts into the realm of what might have been, or even what they think should have been, storytellers evoke a sense of wonder and awe that professional historians all too often fail to inspire. But they do so at a cost.

The reenactors I met on the set of *We Fight to Be Free* take a different approach. Though ignored by academics and sometimes excoriated by filmmakers, they unite an almost fanatical devotion to accuracy with a sincere desire to entertain. There are exceptions. Some George Washington reenactors, or impersonators, play their roles with a view to plying contemporary political or religious agendas. For the most part, however, the average reenactor—the type of person who shares his or her knowledge with schoolchildren and museum and park visitors—has done more to bring history alive with accuracy than any dozen academics or movie producers. Reenactors are not infallible, of course, which is why they often prefer to call themselves "historical interpreters," and unlike academics and filmmakers, they are neither professional researchers nor professional entertainers. The difference is in the sincerity of their outlook. History, they realize, should be both enlightening and fun, but these ingredients don't need to be added—just revealed.

CONCLUSION

GEORGE WASHINGTON IS AN elusive quarry. The closer he seems, the more easily he slips away. Washington fostered this with his own demeanor. Conscious of his role as an actor on the public stage, he crafted an outward persona that obscured his private being. He deliberately hid certain elements of his inner life, and carried them with him to the grave. Even so, he wanted to be known. He preserved the bulk of his correspondence and records, public and private, for posterity, and he fretted endlessly about how his countrymen would remember him after he had gone.

This paradoxical thinking—the wish to be known yet not known—has influenced the search for the real Washington that every generation of Americans has pursued since the founding of the United States. Washington puzzles us. We wish to encounter him as a genuine human being rooted in our culture and history, yet there is this nagging feeling that we might not really like him if we knew him too well. Before exposing Washington to the world with a yank of the curtain and a cry of "voilà," we take a peek behind to make sure he's wearing his clothing, so that if necessary we can toss him a shirt before he steps onstage.

This ambiguity is particularly obvious in the classroom. I come from a family of elementary-school teachers and work regularly with both teachers and schoolchildren in workshops designed to help new generations appreciate Washington and the other Founding Fathers. For the most part, both teachers and children are eager to learn about Washington, but are uncertain how to go about it. Some teachers exalt him into an action hero of the sort that children encounter on Xbox or PlayStation video games, while others promote a mood of lighthearted irreverence by exposing his foibles. Teachers at inner-city schools struggle to address their African-American students' dislike of a man who professed to fight for freedom while holding hundreds of human beings in bondage. All educators are constrained—to their almost universal frustration—by the dictates of state-mandated standards of learning, which require them to emphasize lists of facts, people, and dates rather than use their creativity to help their students appreciate the Founders as people.

For their part, the children do not ask much. They want exciting stories, so long as they are true. They enjoy humorous anecdotes, for they make Washington seem less forbidding. And while they welcome discussions of his weaknesses, I have never met a child who wants to see Washington defamed or torn down. Children want to see a man they can admire but who is also just like them. Simple enough; yet adults tie themselves in knots in attempting to fulfill this request. Part of our problem is that we are always trying to capture Washington in a particular state of being, or frozen at a specific moment in time. He is young or old; a surveyor, farmer, soldier, or president; a son, husband, or stepfather; a man of action, philosopher, or man of God; a bumbler, cynic, or savior. In emphasizing any one element we are always neglecting the rest. More important, we lose sight of the broader nature of his personality. In reality, Washington—like everyone else—moved through life unevenly, facing a multitude of challenges. Sometimes he succeeded in overcoming them, and sometimes he failed. The point that children always can appreciate is that Washington never stopped learning. Kids find it a relief, in fact, to discover that Washington achieved greatness rather than having it handed to him at birth by virtue of divine right.

Adults also benefit from appreciating Washington's life as a journey much like their own, rather than as an immutable monolith. The problem with the statue—or the face on the dollar bill, for that matter—is not that it is tall, cold, or forbidding, but that it is unchanging. People change, and they need him to change with them. And that is the nature of Washington the flesh-and-blood man. In life, he adapted to changing circumstances, grew, and improved. In like manner, the Washington icon, to remain vibrant, must not repeat the same, tired, old deeds generation after generation. Instead, he must stride confidently onward, remodeling himself constantly in the light of shifting conditions, hopes, and needs.

History is always in danger of growing stale through repetition. No one wants to hear the same old tale repeated over again. Discoveries—and rediscoveries—are the imperative stock-in-trade of historians and other storytellers, and rightly so. Unfortunately, the temptation to veer from the straight and narrow in the search for historical truth is well-nigh overwhelming, and nowhere more so than in the search for the truth about George Washington. James Thomas Flexner was wrong to imply that nothing more of value could possibly be uncovered about the great man's life after the comprehensively researched biographies by himself and Douglas Southall Freeman. Even the Papers of George Washington documentary editing project, which is slated for "completion" by about 2025, can never claim to have published every scrap of written evidence pertaining to the Founder. Ultimately, though, the sources of knowledge are finite, and it is not unreasonable to expect that at some point we will have learned just about all that we are ever likely to know about the life of George Washington. What then?

If there is truth in the old cliché that nothing is more constant than the need for change, then it is safe to assume that even the discovery of the last existing Washington letter will not bring the storytelling to an end—providing, that is, that we do not banish the Founder from our memory altogether. As society and circumstances change and new challenges arise, Americans will continue to seek enlightenment and inspiration from Washington's example to the nation. Inevitably, too, we will see things that were never really there, from harmless pink elephants to dangerously misleading will-o'-the-wisps. However much such phantasms obscure our vision, we should never let them divert us from the hunt for truth. There is, after all, joy in the pursuit.

ACKNOWLEDGMENTS

When I arrived at the University of Virginia's Papers of George Washington project in 1996, professor and editor in chief Bill Abbot taught me the trade of documentary editing and set me on the road to professional success. He also inculcated in me a regard and respect for George Washington, and set an example of humanistic scholarship that I will never forget. The idea for this book arose in part from stories that he used to tell about the wild and crazy characters he encountered during his many years at the project. All George Washington scholars are in his debt.

I would also like to thank the editors of the Papers of George Washington project for their professionalism, encouragement, and advice, especially editor in chief Emeritus Ted Crackel; associate editor Bill Ferraro; associate editor David Hoth; assistant editor Ben Huggins; assistant editor Carol Ebel; assistant editor Jennifer Stertzer; and production editor Tom Dulan. All of the opinions stated in this book are my own, however, and do not necessarily reflect the opinions of the staff of the Papers of George Washington. Any mistakes in this book are likewise my own.

The Mount Vernon Ladies' Association has, since its inception in the days of Ann Pamela Cunningham, been dedicated to keeping George Washington alive in American hearts and minds, and doing so with accuracy. I am deeply grateful for the ongoing and always-cheerful cooperation of the Mount Vernon staff, including president James C. Rees; vice president Ann Bay (education); vice president Dennis Pogue (preservation); librarian Mary Thompson; director of programs Nancy Hayward; logistics coordinator Debbie Baker; education associate Laurel Noe; and education associate Meghan Rafferty.

Numerous historians of George Washington and the early American republic have lent their knowledge and advice as I struggled to produce a book that was both readable and informative. These include (in no particular order), Peter Henriques; Ron Chernow; Joe Ellis; John Ferling; Ged Carbone; Tom Fleming; Dick Stazesky; Nelson Lankford; and Rosemarie Zagarri. I would also like to thank my critics—at least the friendly ones!—including writer J. L. Bell of the blog Boston 1775.

At Harper, I am grateful to Elisabeth Dyssegaard for her support in the early stages of his project, and to Bill Strachan and Kathryn Whitenight for seeing it through to completion. My sincere thanks also go out to my agent, Peter Matson of Sterling Lord Literistic.

Personal thanks go to Eleanor Abbot, Mary Anne Andrei, and eminent scholar and man of wisdom James E. Guba. Thanks and love to my wife Laima; my children Mike, Laura, and Tom; my parents Alan and Shelbia; and my devoted miniature dachshund Millie. With their help, I am able to keep even George Washington's towering presence in perspective.

BIBLIOGRAPHY

Alderman, Edwin Anderson, et al., eds. *Library of Southern Literature*. New Orleans: Martin and Hoyt, 1907.

Barber, John W. *Historical Collections of New Jersey: Past and Present: Containing a General Collection of the Most Interesting Facts, Traditions, Biographical Sketches, Anecdotes, etc., Relating to the History and Antiquities, with Geographical Descriptions of All the Important Places in the State, and the State Census of All the Towns in 1865*. New Haven, CT: John W. Barber, 1868.

Beck, Henry Charlton. *The Roads of Home: Lanes and Legends of New Jersey*. New Brunswick, NJ: Rutgers University Press, 1956.

Boudinot, Elias. *Journal or Historical Recollections of American Events During the Revolutionary War*. Philadelphia: F. Bourquin, 1894.

Browder, Laura. *Her Best Shot: Women and Guns in America*. Chapel Hill: University of North Carolina Press, 2008.

Bruggeman, Seth C. *Here, George Washington Was Born: Memory, Material Culture, and the Public History of a National Monument*. Athens: University of Georgia Press, 2008.

Bryan, William Alfred. *George Washington in American Literature, 1775–1865*. New York: Columbia University Press, 1952.

Bryant, Linda Allen. *I Cannot Tell a Lie: The True Story of George Washington's African American Descendants*. New York: iUniverse Star, 2001.

Burk, William Herbert. *Washington's Prayers*. Norristown, PA, 1907.

Cleman, John. "Irresistible Impulses: Edgar A. Poe and the Insanity Defense." *American Literature* 63, 4 (December 1991): 623–40.

Coleman, Christopher K. *Ghosts and Haunts of the Civil War: Authentic Accounts of the Strange and Unexplained*. Nashville: Rutledge Hill Press, 1999.

Conkling, Ira B. *The Conklings in America*. Washington, DC: Charles H. Potter, 1913.

Connell, Janice. *Faith of Our Founding Father: The Spiritual Journey of George Washington*. New York: Hatherleigh Press, 2004.

Cooper, Susan Fenimore. *Mount Vernon: A Letter to the Children of America*. New York: D. Appleton, 1858.

Crackel, Theodore J. "Jared Sparks and the Washington Papers." Morristown National Historical Park website, www.nps.gov/archive/morr/Sparks/Sparks_Letters/Sparks/Welcome.htm, accessed October 10, 2009.

Craven, Wesley Frank. *The Legend of the Founding Fathers*. New York: New York University Press, 1956.

Cunliffe, Marcus. *George Washington: Man and Monument*. Boston: Little, Brown, 1958.

———. *In Search of America: Transatlantic Essays, 1951–1990*. New York: Greenwood Press, 1991.

Custis, George Washington Parke. *Recollections and Private Memoirs of Washington, by His Adopted Son, George Washington Parke Custis, with a Memoir of the Author, by His Daughter; and Illustrative and Explanatory Notes*. Ed. Bernard Lossing. New York: Derby and Jackson, 1860.

Darrach, Henry. *Lydia Darragh: One of the Heroines of the Revolution*. Philadelphia: The Society, 1916.

DeGrazia, Emilio. "Poe's Devoted Democrat, George Lippard." *Poe Studies* VI, 1 (June 1973): 6–8.

Earle, Alice Morse. *Colonial Dames and Good Wives*. Boston: Houghton Mifflin, 1896.

Elkins, Stanley, and Eric McKitrick. *The Age of Federalism*. New York: Oxford University Press, 1993.

Ellis, Edith. *An Autobiography of George Washington, As Told to Edith Ellis, Scribe*. Carlsbad, CA: Hay House, 2005.

Everitt, Charles P. *The Adventures of a Treasure Hunter: A Rare Bookman in Search of American History*. Boston: Little, Brown, 1951.

Falkner, Leonard. "A Spy for Washington." *American Heritage* 8, 5 (August 1957): 58–64.

Farington, Joseph. *The Farington Diary*. Ed. James Grieg. 8 vols. New York: George H. Doran, 1923–28.

Fitzpatrick, John C. *George Washington Himself: A Common-Sense Biography Written from His Manuscripts*. Indianapolis: Bobbs-Merrill, 1930.

———. *The George Washington Scandals*. Alexandria, VA: Washington Society of Alexandria, 1929.

Flexner, James Thomas. *George Washington*. 4 vols. Boston: Little, Brown, 1965–72.

———. *Maverick's Progress: An Autobiography*. New York: Fordham University Press, 1996.

Ford, Paul Leicester. *The True George Washington*. Philadelphia: J. B. Lippincott, 1896.

Ford, Worthington Chauncey. *The Spurious Letters Attributed to Washington: With a Bibliographical Note*. Brooklyn, NY, 1889.

Freeman, Douglas Southall. *George Washington: A Biography*. 7 vols. New York: Charles Scribner's Sons, 1948–57.

Friedman, Lawrence J. *Inventors of the Promised Land*. New York: Knopf, 1975.

Glenn, Thomas Allen. *Some Colonial Mansions and Those Who Lived in Them*. Philadelphia: Henry T. Coates, 1900.

Goodman, Matthew. *The Sun and the Moon: The Remarkable True Account of Hoaxers, Showmen, Dueling Journalists, and Lunar Man-Bats in Nineteenth-Century New York*. New York: Basic Books, 2008.

Goolrick, John T. *Fredericksburg and the Cavalier Country, America's Most Historic Section: Its Homes, Its People and Romances.* Richmond, VA: Garrett and Massic, 1935.

———. *Historic Fredericksburg: The Story of an Old Town.* Richmond, VA: Whittet and Shepperson, 1922.

Gordon, William. *The History of the Rise, Progress, and Establishment, of the Independence of the United States of America: Including an Account of the Late War; and of the Thirteen Colonies, from their Origin to that Period.* 4 vols. London: Charles Dilly and James Buckland, 1788.

Greene, Nathanael. *The Papers of General Nathanael Greene.* Ed. Richard K. Showman et al. 13 vols. Chapel Hill: University of North Carolina Press, 1976–2005.

Griswold, Rufus Wilmot. *The Republican Court, or, American Society in the Days of Washington.* Rev ed. New York: D. Appleton, 1856. (Orig. pub. 1854.)

Grizzard, Frank E., Jr. *George Washington: A Biographical Companion.* Santa Barbara, CA: ABC-CLIO, 2002.

———. *143 Questions & Answers About George Washington.* Buena Vista, VA: Mariner, 2009.

———. *The Ways of Providence: Religion & George Washington.* Buena Vista, VA: Mariner, 2005.

Hall, Manly P. *The Secret Destiny of America.* Los Angeles: Philosophical Research Society, 1944.

Harvey, Frederick L. *History of the Washington National Monument and of the Washington National Monument Society.* Washington, DC: Norman T. Elliott, 1902.

Henriques, Peter R. *Realistic Visionary: A Portrait of George Washington.* Charlottesville: University of Virginia Press, 2006.

Honeyman, A. Van Doren. *The Honeyman Family (Honeyman, Honyman, Hunneman, Etc.) in Scotland and America 1548–1908.* Plainfield, NJ: Honeyman's, 1909.

Hosack, David. *Memoir of DeWitt Clinton: With Illustrations of the Principal Events of His Life.* New York, 1829.

Hughes, Rupert. *George Washington*. 3 vols. New York: William Morrow, 1926–30.

Humphreys, David. *David Humphreys' Life of General Washington: With George Washington's "Remarks."* Ed. Rosemarie Zagarri. Athens: University of Georgia Press, 1991.

Irving, Washington. *Life of George Washington*. Eds. Allen Guttmann and James A. Sappenfield. 3 vols. Boston: Twayne, 1982. (Orig. pub. 1857, in 5 vols.)

Johnson, David E. *Douglas Southall Freeman*. Gretna, LA: Pelican, 2002.

Johnstone, William J. *George Washington the Christian*. New York: Abingdon Press, 1919.

Kahler, Gerald E. *The Long Farewell: Americans Mourn the Death of George Washington*. Charlottesville: University of Virginia Press, 2008.

———. "Washington in Glory, America in Tears: The Nation Mourns the Death of George Washington, 1799–1800." Ph.D. diss., College of William and Mary, 2003.

Kaminski, John P., and Jill Adair McCaughan, eds. *A Great and Good Man: George Washington in the Eyes of His Contemporaries*. Madison, WI: Madison House, 1989.

Kammen, Michael G. *A Season of Youth: The American Revolution and the Historical Imagination*. New York: Knopf, 1978.

Kemm, James O. *Rupert Hughes: A Hollywood Legend*. Beverly Hills, CA: Pomegranate Press, 1997.

Ketchum, Richard. *The Winter Soldiers*. Garden City, NY: Doubleday, 1973.

Kirkland, Caroline Matilda. *Memoirs of Washington*. New York: D. Appleton, 1857.

Krensky, Stephen. *Hanukkah at Valley Forge*. New York: Dutton, 2006.

LaHaye, Tim. *Faith of Our Founding Fathers*. Green Forest, AR: Master Books, 1990.

Lengel, Edward G. *General George Washington*. New York: Random House, 2005.

Libby, Orin Grant. "A Critical Examination of William Gordon's History of the American Revolution." *Annual Report of the American Historical Association* 1 (1899): 365–88.

Lippard, George. *Paul Ardenheim: The Monk of Wissahikon.* Philadelphia: T. B. Peterson, 1848.

———. *The Quaker City, or, The Monks of Monk Hall: A Romance of Philadelphia Life, Mystery, and Crime.* Ed. David S. Reynolds. Amherst: University of Massachusetts Press, 1995.

———. *Washington and His Generals: or, Legends of the Revolution.* Philadelphia: G. B. Zieber, 1847.

———. *Washington and His Men: A New Series of Legends of the Revolution.* Philadelphia: Joseph Severns, 1849.

Lodge, Henry Cabot. *The Life of George Washington.* 2 vols. Boston: Houghton Mifflin, 1920. (Orig. pub. 1889.)

Lossing, Bernard. *The Pictorial Field-Book of the Revolution.* 2 vols. New York: Harper and Brothers, 1851–52.

Madison, James. *The Writings of James Madison.* Ed. Gaillard Hunt. 9 vols. New York: G. P. Putnam's Sons, 1900–10.

Marling, Karal Ann. *George Washington Slept Here: Colonial Revivals and American Culture, 1876–1986.* Cambridge, MA: Harvard University Press, 1988.

McCullough, David. *1776.* New York: Simon and Schuster, 2005.

McGuffey, William Holmes. *The Eclectic Second Reader; Consisting of Progressive Lessons in Reading and Spelling.* Cincinnati: Truman and Smith, 1836.

Meade, William. *Old Churches, Ministers and Families of Virginia.* 2 vols. Philadelphia: Lippincott, 1910. (Orig. pub. 1857.)

M'Guire, E. C. *The Religious Opinions and Character of Washington.* New York: Harper and Brothers, 1836.

Paine, Thomas. *Thomas Paine: Representative Selections.* Ed. Harry Hayden Clark. New York: American Book Company, 1944.

Pilcher, George William. "William Gordon and the History of the American Revolution." *The Historian* 34, 3 (May 1972): 447–64.

Pogue, Dennis. "Beyond Mansion and Myth: Expanding Interpretation of a National Shrine." Paper presented at the annual conference of the Association for Living History, Farms, and Agricultural Museums, Williamsburg, VA, June 13, 2001.

Pullen, John J. *The Twentieth Maine: A Volunteer Regiment in the Civil War.* Dayton, OH: Morningside Bookshop, 1984. (Orig. pub. 1957.)

Raphael, Ray. *Founding Myths: Stories That Hide Our Patriotic Past.* New York: New Press, 2004.

Reiss, Benjamin. *The Showman and the Slave: Race, Death, and Memory in Barnum's America.* Cambridge, MA: Harvard University Press, 2001.

Remsburg, John. *Six Historic Americans: Paine, Jefferson, Washington, Franklin, Lincoln, Grant, the Fathers and Saviors of Our Republic, Freethinkers.* New York: Truth Seeker, 1906.

Reynolds, David S. *George Lippard.* Boston: Twayne, 1982.

Rush, Benjamin. *The Autobiography of Benjamin Rush: His "Travels Through Life" Together with His Commonplace Book for 1789–1813.* Ed. George W. Corner. Princeton: Princeton University Press, 1948.

Schwartz, Barry. *George Washington: The Making of an American Symbol.* New York: Free Press, 1987.

Slaughter, Philip. *Christianity the Key to the Character and Career of Washington.* New York: Thomas Whittaker, 1886.

Smith, Susy. *Prominent American Ghosts.* Cleveland: World, 1967.

Steiner, Franklin. *The Religious Beliefs of Our Presidents.* Girard, KS: Haldeman-Julius, 1936.

Stryker, William S. *The Battles of Trenton and Princeton.* Spartanburg, SC: Reprint Co., 1967. (Orig. pub. 1898.)

Tagg, James D. "Benjamin Franklin Bache's Attack on George Washington." *Pennsylvania Magazine of History and Biography* 100 (1976): 191–230.

Thane, Elswyth. *Mount Vernon Is Ours: The Story of Its Preservation.* New York: Duell, Sloane, and Pierce, 1966.

Twohig, Dorothy. "George Washington Forgeries and Facsimiles." *Provenance: The Journal of the Society of Georgia Archivists* 1 (Spring 1983): 1–13.

Washington, George. *The Papers of George Washington.* Ed. W. W. Abbot et al. 5 ser., 61 vols. to date. Charlottesville: University of Virginia Press, 1983–.

——. *The Writings of George Washington from the Original Manuscript Sources, 1745–1799.* Ed. John C. Fitzpatrick. 39 vols. Washington, DC: U.S. Government Printing Office, 1931–44.

Washington, Lawrence, et al. *Westmoreland County Virginia, 1653–1912.* Richmond, VA: Whittet and Shepperson, 1912.

Weems, Mason Locke. *The Life of Washington: A New Edition with Primary Documents and Introduction by Peter S. Onuf.* Armonk, NY: M. E. Sharpe, 1996.

Wharton, Anne Hollingsworth. *Colonial Days and Dames.* Philadelphia: J. B. Lippincott, 1895.

White, Virgil D. *Genealogical Abstracts of Revolutionary War Pension Files.* 4 vols. Waynesboro, TN: National Historical Publishing, 1992.

Wick, Wendy C. *George Washington, an American Icon: The Eighteenth-Century Graphic Portraits.* Washington, DC: Smithsonian Institution Traveling Exhibition Service, 1982.

Wills, Garry. *Cincinnatus: George Washington and the Enlightenment.* Garden City, NY: Doubleday, 1984.

Woodward, William E. *George Washington: The Image and the Man.* London: Jonathan Cape, 1928.

——. *The Gift of Life: An Autobiography.* New York: E. P. Dutton, 1947.

NOTES

Chapter 1: Washington Lives, Dies, and Is Reborn

1. Ford, *Spurious Letters Attributed to Washington*, 5–120.
2. *Papers of George Washington* (henceforth PGW), *Revolutionary War Series*, 15:216, 269.
3. Tagg, "Benjamin Franklin Bache's Attack on George Washington," 191, 209, 211; *Thomas Paine*, 391, 399, 402, 404, 408.
4. *Writings of Washington*, 35:414; Ford, *Spurious Letters*, 16–28; Elkins and McKitrick, *Age of Federalism*, 415–26; Tagg, 221.
5. *Autobiography of Benjamin Rush*, 113.
6. *Writings of Washington*, 26:336.
7. Lengel, *General George Washington*, 352.
8. Wills, *Cincinnatus*, 13; Kaminski and McCaughan, eds., *A Great and Good Man*, 36–44.
9. Farington, *Farington Diary*, 1:279.
10. Kurt Soller, "The Man Who Would Be King," Newsweek .com, October 8, 2008. In May 1782, Colonel Lewis Nicola wrote to Washington that America might need to adopt a more authoritarian constitution after the war ended. "Some people have so connected the ideas of tyranny & monarchy

as to find it very difficult to separate [*sic*] them," he wrote, "[and] it may therefore be requisite to give the head of such a constitution as I propose some title apparently more moderate, but if all other things were once adjusted I believe strong arguments might be produced for admitting the title of king, which I conceive would be attended with some material advantages." Nicola spoke entirely on his behalf, but the mere suggestion infuriated Washington, who replied expressing his "abhorrence" for everything that the colonel had written. Washington later admitted that he had received "several applications" along the same lines—all, evidently, from cranks—but he never took any of them seriously (PGW, *Presidential Series*, 1:2–4, 200–1). As James Madison wrote in 1826, "I am not less sure that General Washington would have spurned a sceptre if within his grasp, than I am that it was out of his reach, if he had secretly sighed for it" (*Writings of James Madison*, 9:251).

11. PGW, *Retirement Series*, 4:542–52.
12. Kahler, "Washington in Glory, America in Tears," 41–42.
13. Grizzard, *Ways of Providence*, 2; Kahler, *Long Farewell*, 59–62.
14. Kahler, "Washington in Glory, America in Tears," 46; Friedman, *Inventors of the Promised Land*, 58–59.
15. Kahler, *Long Farewell*, 21–37, 49, 62, 83.
16. PGW, *Retirement Series*, 4:500; *Writings of Washington*, 25:287–89; *David Humphreys' Life of General Washington*, xviii–xix, xxix–xxxi.
17. Crackel, "Jared Sparks and the Washington Papers"; PGW, *Diaries*, 1:xlii–xliv; PGW, *Colonial Series*, 1:xiv–xv; *Pittsfield* (Massachusetts) *Sun*, April 10, 1951.
18. Weems, *Life of Washington*, xix.
19. Weems, xix; Grizzard, *Ways of Providence*, 45–47; PGW, *Diaries*, 5:112.
20. Weems, ix.
21. Quoted in Bryan, *George Washington in American Literature*, 14.

22. Weems, 2–3.
23. Weems, 5–14.
24. Quoted in Grizzard, *Ways of Providence*, 19–20; Weems, xvii; Wills, 50.
25. Lodge, *The Life of George Washington*, 1:42–43.
26. Quoted in Grizzard, *George Washington*, 46.
27. Grizzard, *George Washington*, 46; Wills, 52–53; Weems, 11–13; McGuffey, *The Eclectic Second Reader*, 126–31.
28. Bryan, 70–71; Friedman, 46–51, 76.

CHAPTER 2: WASHINGTON TURNS A PROFIT

1. Reiss, *Showman and the Slave*, 17–21.
2. Reiss, 29–37.
3. Quoted in Reiss, 63.
4. Reiss, 75–81.
5. Reiss, 88–115.
6. Reiss, 135–67; Goodman, *Sun and the Moon*, 257–58.
7. PGW, *Confederation Series*, 2:116; Grizzard, *George Washington*, 64.
8. PGW, *Retirement Series*, 1:153.
9. Bruggeman, *Here, George Washington Was Born*, 25.
10. Grizzard, *George Washington*, 157.
11. *Recollections and Private Memoirs of Washington*, 133–34, 141, 225, 286–87, 483–84.
12. Ibid., 489–94.
13. DeGrazia, "Poe's Devoted Democrat," 6–8.
14. Lippard, *Quaker City*, vii, xii–xiii; Cleman, "Irresistible Impulses," 626.
15. Reynolds, *George Lippard*, 8–9, 12, 14, 31.
16. Quoted in Bryan, 16; quoted in Wills, 68.
17. Lippard, *Washington and His Generals*, 51–52.
18. Lippard, *Paul Ardenheim*, 158–65.
19. Lippard, *Quaker City*, xxx.

20. "The Mystical George Washington," http://www.reversespins .com/mysticalwashington.html.

21. Lippard, *Washington and His Generals*, 107–11, 394–96; Reynolds, 64–66; "The Unknown Patriot," article in Thomas Jefferson Encyclopedia, http://wiki.monticello.org/mediawiki/ index.php/Thomas_Jefferson_Encyclopedia.

22. Information on Spring forgeries and others maintained internally by the Papers of George Washington documentary editing project; see also Twohig, "George Washington Forgeries and Facsimiles," 1–13.

CHAPTER 3: WASHINGTON'S LOVES

1. PGW, *Revolutionary War Series*, 15:483.

2. *Papers of General Nathanael Greene*, 3:354.

3. "A Washington Affair of Honor, 1779," *Pennsylvania Magazine of History and Biography* 65, 3 (July 1941): 362–70.

4. PGW, *Colonial Series*, 1:40–41, 46–47.

5. PGW, *Colonial Series*, 1:203–4.

6. PGW, *Colonial Series*, 1:346.

7. Freeman, *George Washington*, 2:160.

8. PGW, *Colonial Series*, 6:10–13; Henriques, *Realistic Visionary*, 79–80.

9. Henriques, *Realistic Visionary*, 87.

10. PGW, *Confederation Series*, 4:134–35.

11. PGW, *Confederation Series*, 2:196–97.

12. Kirkland, *Memoirs of Washington*, 32–33, 49–50, 87, 165, 176–77; Bryan, 106–7.

13. Meade, *Old Churches, Ministers and Families of Virginia*, 1:108–9.

14. "A Little Centennial Lady," *Scribner's Monthly*, 12, 3 (July 1876): 301–11.

15. Conway, "Footprints in Washingtonland," *Harper's New*

Monthly Magazine, April 1889, 738–44; "Washington as Lover and Poet," *Harper's Weekly*, May 4, 1889, 343.

16. Ford, *The True George Washington*, 93–94, 105–7.
17. Marling, *George Washington Slept Here*, 143.
18. Lodge, 1:100.
19. Glenn, *Some Colonial Mansions*, 271.
20. Quoted in Marling, 146.
21. Valerie Hope, "The Love Affairs of George Washington," *Belleville News Democrat*, February 22, 1908.
22. Frederic J. Haskin, "Stories of George Washington," *Omaha World Herald*, February 22, 1907.
23. Quoted in Marling, 141–42.
24. Quoted in Marling, 145.
25. Marling, 187–90, 249–50.
26. Woodward, *George Washington*, 33–36; Hughes, *George Washington*, 1:190.
27. Fitzpatrick, *The George Washington Scandals*, 9.
28. Brigid Schulte, "Fresh Look at Martha Washington: Less First Frump, More Foxy Lady," *Washington Post*, February 2, 2009.

Chapter 4: Washington's Visions

1. Everitt, *Adventures of a Treasure Hunter*, 200.
2. *New York Times*, February 12, 1891.
3. Burk, *Washington's Prayers*, 13–14.
4. Burk, 15.
5. The editors of the Papers of George Washington documentary editing project at the University of Virginia, with well over a hundred years' combined experience studying Washington's handwriting, have always concurred in this conclusion; see also Grizzard, *The Ways of Providence*, 51–55.
6. Burk, 15–17.

7. Henriques, "'A Sly Old Fox'? George Washington and Religion," speech to the Mount Vernon Teachers' Institute, July 21, 1999; LaHaye, *Faith of Our Founding Fathers*, 113; Jim Manship, "Prayer Warrior," http://prayerwarriorwashington.blogspot.com.

8. Bryan, 17.

9. Slaughter, *Christianity the Key to the Character and Career of Washington*, 29, 33.

10. Hannity's speech is viewable on YouTube, and the transcript of Beck's TV program is available at www.foxnews.com; see also Bruce Wilson, "How Fake American History Feeds Christian Nationalism," http://www.talk2action.org/story/2008/1/5/155457/0298.

11. *Writings of Washington*, 26:496. The false transcription appears on dozens of websites; the original manuscript is in the Pierpont Morgan Library, New York.

12. Hughes, 3:290–92; Wilson, "How Fake American History Feeds Christian Nationalism."

13. Lengel, 105; J. L. Bell, "Washington Reads the 101st Psalm?" Boston 1775 Blog, October 21, 2007.

14. "Washington's Baptism," *Time*, September 5, 1932; "The John Gano Evidence of George Washington's Religion," *Bulletin of William Jewell College*, September 15, 1926; "George Washington and His Character," http://www.elliottbaptist.org/sermons/2007/psa33–12.pdf.

15. "Remarks at a White House Ceremony in Observance of National Day of Prayer," May 6, 1982, http://www.reagan.utexas.edu/archives/speeches/1982/50682c.htm.

16. Marling, 3.

17. Grizzard, *The Ways of Providence*, 19–24.

18. M'Guire, *Religious Opinions and Character of Washington*, 158–70.

19. Lossing, *Pictorial Field-Book of the Revolution*, 2:336.

20. Gilbert Starling Jones, "Prayer of Valley Forge May be Legend

or Tradition or a Fact, Yet it Remains Symbol of Faith," *Picket Post* 9 (April 1945).

21. "Washington's Prayer," *New York Times*, February 22, 1895.
22. Hughes, 3:281–2; Steiner, *Religious Beliefs of Our Presidents*, 15.
23. Charles Colson, "Why Washington is 'The Father of Our Country,'" http://www.cbn.com/spirituallife/churchandmin istry/churchhistory/why_washington_is_the_father_of_our_ country.aspx; Family Research Council, http://www.frc.org/ prayerteam/prayer-team-targets-christmas-1776-2008.
24. Marling, 1–8.
25. *New York Times*, February 14, March 23, 1907; Marling, 6.
26. http://www.nps.gov/vafo/historyculture/treese8a.htm.
27. Jones, "Prayer of Valley Forge."
28. Conkling, *The Conklings in America*, 112; Hosack, *Memoir of DeWitt Clinton*, 183–84.
29. Johnstone, *George Washington the Christian*, 89.
30. Johnstone, 89–90.
31. J. L. Bell, "Washington's Hanukkah: An Oral Tradition," Boston 1775 Blog, February 7, 2007; Penny Schwartz, "By George, it's a New Spin on Hanukkah," *Boston Globe*, December 10, 2006.
32. *Philadelphia Inquirer*, June 24, 1861.
33. *Newark Advocate*, February 28, 1862.
34. Browder, *Her Best Shot*, 31–32.
35. White, *Genealogical Abstracts of Revolutionary War Pension Files*, 3:3108; *DAR Patriot Index, Centennial Edition*, 3:2644.
36. *Deseret Evening News*, Feb 1–2, 1877.
37. *National Tribune* 4, 12 (December 1880); Grizzard, *143 Questions and Answers About George Washington*, 83–85.
38. Smith, *Prominent American Ghosts*, 75; Grizzard, *143 Questions and Answers*, 83–85; see also, for example, David M. Balmforth, *America's Coming Crisis: Prophetic Warnings, Divine Destiny* (Bountiful, UT: Horizon, 1998), 66–72.

39. Connell, *Faith of Our Founding Father,* 121–34, 166–67, 193.
40. Remsburg, *Six Historic Americans,* 110–11.
41. Woodward, *George Washington,* 143.
42. Hughes, 1:476, 552–59.
43. Woodward, *George Washington,* 266.
44. McCullough, *John Adams* (New York: Simon and Schuster, 2008), 387; Kenneth C. Davis, *Don't Know Much About History: Everything You Need to Know About American History but Never Learned* (New York: HarperCollins, 2007), 131; "So Help Me God: A Historical Look at the Inauguration," http://inaugural.senate.gov/history/video/video-sohelpmegod.cfm; Peter R. Henriques, "'So Help Me God': A George Washington Myth That Should Be Discarded," History News Network, http://hnn.us/articles/59548.html.
45. Sidney P. Moss, *Poe's Literary Battles: The Critic in the Context of His Literary Milieu* (Durham: Duke University Press, 1963), 80–81.
46. Griswold, *The Republican Court,* 141.
47. Irving, *Life of George Washington,* 2:287.
48. Henriques, "'So Help Me God.'"
49. *Washington Post,* January 18, 2009.

Chapter 5: Washington Slept Here

1. *San Jose Evening News,* February 21, 1911.
2. *Independent Chronicle and Boston Patriot,* September 4, 1824.
3. *Salem Gazette,* August 19, 1828.
4. *Philadelphia Inquirer,* July 4, 1897.
5. Beck, *The Roads of Home,* 48–62; *New York Times,* July 28, 1889.
6. Townsend Ward, "A Walk to Darby," *Pennsylvania Magazine of History and Biography* 3, 3 (1879): 264.
7. Goolrick, *Historic Fredericksburg,* 70.
8. Goolrick, *Fredericksburg and the Cavalier Country,* 31.

9. Bruggeman, 26, 51–53, 64–75, 86–113.

10. *Daily Picayune*, May 28, 1871.

11. Thane, *Mount Vernon Is Ours*, 342–43.

12. Quoted in Marling, 76–77.

13. Cooper, *Mount Vernon*, 70.

14. Marling, 83–84.

15. Pogue, "Beyond Mansion and Myth," 6–7; email from Pogue to the author, November 12, 2009.

16. Marling, 70–71.

17. Harvey, *History of the Washington National Monument*, 95–111.

18. *Telegraph and Messenger* (Macon, GA), February 1, 1885.

19. *Magazine of American History* 8, 1 (1882): 205; *Philadelphia Inquirer*, October 6, 1881.

20. *New Haven Evening Register*, February 4, 1885; *Telegraph and Messenger* (Macon, GA), February 11, 1885.

21. Quoted in Marling, 74.

22. *Morning Oregonian*, November 19, 1922.

23. *San Francisco Evening Bulletin*, December 14, 1871.

24. Barber, *Historical Collections of New Jersey*, 296–97, 386.

25. "Notes and Queries," *Pennsylvania Magazine of History and Biography* 8, 4 (1884): 431.

26. "Notes and Queries," *Pennsylvania Magazine of History and Biography* 6, 4 (1882): 488.

27. *American Quarterly Review* 1 (March 1827): 25–27; see also Lossing, *Pictorial Field-Book of the Revolution*, 2:301–2.

28. *American Quarterly Review* 1 (March 1827): 25–27.

29. Boudinot, *Journal or Historical Recollections*, 50–53.

30. Quoted in Darrach, *Lydia Darragh*, 394.

31. William Canby, "The History of the Flag of the United States," http://www.ushistory.org/betsy/more/canby.htm.

32. Grizzard, *143 Questions and Answers*, 17–18; http://www.betsyrosshouse.org.

33. Stryker, *The Battles of Trenton and Princeton*, 87–89; Leonard Falkner, "A Spy for Washington," *American Heritage* 8, 5

(August 1957): 58–64; John Van Dyke, "An Unwritten Account of a Spy of Washington," *Our Home: A Monthly Magazine of Original Articles*, October 1873, 445–52; Ketchum, *Winter Soldiers*, 288–89; see also Honeyman, *Honeyman Family*.

34. Quoted in Alderman, *Library of Southern Literature*, 16:143.
35. Washington, *Westmoreland County Virginia*, 65–66.
36. PGW, *Revolutionary War Series*, 3:386. Thanks to Ron Chernow for pointing out this letter to me.
37. Gordon, *History*, 2:354.
38. Libby, "A Critical Examination of William Gordon's History of the American Revolution," 383; Pilcher, "William Gordon and the History of the American Revolution," 462.

Chapter 6: Washington Debunked

1. Woodward, *Gift of Life*, 233–45.
2. Woodward, *Gift of Life*, 292, 296, 321.
3. Woodward, *George Washington*, 11–24, 311.
4. Woodward, *George Washington*, 45–51, 244, 250–51.
5. Woodward, *George Washington*, 67, 78, 255, 287, 334–35, 342, 348, 356.
6. "Washington 'Dismounted from His High Horse,'" *Literary Digest*, December 12, 1925, 50–52.
7. "Washington—Man or Waxwork?" *Nation*, January 27, 1926, 75.
8. Kemm, *Rupert Hughes*, 117.
9. Kemm, *Rupert Hughes*, 155.
10. Hughes, *George Washington*, 2:8.
11. Hughes, *George Washington*, 1:54–55.
12. Hughes, *George Washington*, 2:584, 650.
13. Hughes, *George Washington*, 1:488–89, 2:607.
14. Kemm, *Rupert Hughes*, 290.
15. Steiner, 15.
16. Marling, 295–98.

17. Marling, 365.
18. Wills, 39–41; Marling, 335–46.
19. Wills, xxiii–xxiv. This myth dated from the mid-nineteenth century but attained popularity only after the debunkers passed through.
20. Fitzpatrick, *George Washington Himself*, xi.
21. Fitzpatrick, *George Washington Himself*, 19.
22. Marling, 362.
23. Marling, 327–36, 356.
24. Kammen, *A Season of Youth*, 287.
25. Marling, 374–76.

CHAPTER 7: THE INDISPENSABLE MAN

1. Marling, 376.
2. Flexner, *Maverick's Progress*, 19.
3. Flexner, *Maverick's Progress*, 95–101.
4. Flexner, *Maverick's Progress*, 197.
5. Flexner, *Maverick's Progress*, 237.
6. Flexner, *Maverick's Progress*, 237–38.
7. Flexner, *Maverick's Progress*, 257–59.
8. Flexner, *Maverick's Progress*, 317–23.
9. Flexner, *Maverick's Progress*, 384–85.
10. Johnson, *Douglas Southall Freeman*, 61.
11. Johnson, *Douglas Southall Freeman*, 113.
12. Johnson, *Douglas Southall Freeman*, 232.
13. Johnson, *Douglas Southall Freeman*, 303–4.
14. Johnson, *Douglas Southall Freeman*, 307, 338.
15. Johnson, *Douglas Southall Freeman*, 66.
16. Flexner, *Maverick's Progress*, 390.
17. Flexner, *Maverick's Progress*, 389.
18. Flexner, *Maverick's Progress*, 385–400.
19. Flexner, *George Washington*, 1:31, 38, 47.
20. Flexner, *George Washington*, 1:75.

21. Flexner, *George Washington*, 1:87.
22. Flexner, *George Washington*, 1:132.
23. Flexner, *George Washington*, 2:69; McCullough, *1776*, 86.
24. *New York Times*, February 16, 2003.
25. Flexner, *Maverick's Progress*, 455–56.
26. Flexner, *Maverick's Progress*, 405.
27. Flexner, *Maverick's Progress*, 483.
28. Flexner, *Maverick's Progress*, 487.
29. Flexner, *Maverick's Progress*, 495, 501.

Chapter 8: The Living Myth

1. Ellis, *An Autobiography of George Washington*, 12.
2. Ellis, *An Autobiography of George Washington*, 20.
3. See Caroline Myss website at http://myss.com.
4. Ellis, *An Autobiography of George Washington*, 36.
5. Ellis, *An Autobiography of George Washington*, 39–51.
6. Ellis, *An Autobiography of George Washington*, 55, 101–112, 150–57.
7. Ellis, *An Autobiography of George Washington*, 23–27, 172–73, 181, 201, 208, 305.
8. Ellis, *An Autobiography of George Washington*, 305–6, 322–23, 366.
9. Ellis, *An Autobiography of George Washington*, 255.
10. Grizzard, *143 Questions and Answers*, 49.
11. Bryant, *I Cannot Tell a Lie*, xii.
12. Bryant, 15, 18.
13. Bryant, 13.
14. Bryant, xii–xiii.
15. Volta website (no longer available as of 2010).
16. This quotation may be found on dozens of websites.
17. Grizzard, *143 Questions and Answers*, 37–38.
18. For example, see Ed Rosenthal and Steve Kubby, *Why Marijuana Should be Legal* (New York: Thunder's Mouth Press,

2003), 43; the quotation also appears on numerous pro-cannabis websites. GW did advise his farm manager to "let the most that can be made of the pint of Oats which the Gardener raised last year, and of the hemp seed," in the context of urging agricultural economy, but he did not write "sow it everywhere," which is a modern addition (*Writings of Washington*, 33:243).

19. Email, October 23, 1998, in author's possession.
20. "Tommy Franks/George Washington," Return of the Revolutionaries website, http://www.johnadams.net/cases/samples/Franks-Washington/index.html.
21. *New York Times*, March 7, 1877.
22. *Fort Worth Morning Register*, September 29, 1897; *Telegraph and Register* (Macon, GA), November 26, 1881; *Aberdeen Daily News*, May 19, 1891.
23. Coleman, *Ghosts and Haunts of the Civil War*, 16–17.
24. "Ghosts and Spirits Roam Our Streets," *Alexandria Times*, October 27, 2005.
25. Coleman, 72.
26. *Hearst's Magazine*, June 1913, 894–909.
27. Pullen, *The Twentieth Maine*, 242.
28. Pullen, 242–43.

INDEX